FEARON'S
Economics
SECOND EDITION

FEARON'S

Economics

SECOND EDITION

Jane S. Lopus, Ph.D.
Marna Owen

GLOBE FEARON
EDUCATIONAL PUBLISHER
PARAMUS, NEW JERSEY

Paramount Publishing

Pacemaker Curriculum Advisor: Stephen C. Larsen

Stephen C. Larsen holds a B.S. and an M.S. in Speech Pathology from the University of Nebraska at Omaha, and Ed.D. in Learning Disabilities from the University of Kansas. In the course of his career, Dr. Larsen has worked in the Teacher Corps on a Nebraska Indian Reservation, as a Fulbright senior lecturer in Portugal and Spain, and as a speech pathologist in the public schools. A full professor at the University of Texas at Austin, he has nearly twenty years' experience as a teacher trainer on the university level. He is the author of sixty journal articles, three textbooks, and six widely used standardized tests including the Test of Written Learning (TOWL) and the Test of Adolescent Language (TOAL).

The Authors: Jane S. Lopus, Ph.D., and Marna Owen

Jane S. Lopus received a Ph.D. in Economics from the University of California, Davis in 1990. She is currently Assistant Professor of Economics and Director of the Center for Economic Education at California State University, Hayward. She also holds an M.S. in Special Education and is a former high school teacher of economics and special education.

Marna Owen is a well-known West Coast writer and instructional designer who specializes in educational and training materials. She has written numerous texts and supporting materials in the areas of health, English, economics, history, and government.

Subject Area Consultant: Don R. Leet, Ph.D.

Don R. Leet holds a Ph.D. in Economics from the University of Pennsylvania. He is currently Professor of Economics and Director of the Center for Economic Education at California State University, Fresno. In 1990, he was President of the National Association of Economic Educators.

Supervising Editor: Stephen Feinstein
Text Designer: Diane Platner
Cover Designer/Graphics Coordinator: Joe C. Shines
Managing Editors: Ellie Trautman, Renée Beach
Production Managers: Teresa A. Holden, Penny Gibson
Production Editors: Teresa R. Thomas, Nicole Cypher
Desktop Specialist: Eric Dawson
Marketing Manager: Marge Curson
Photo Researcher: Anna M. Smith

Photo Credits: See page 327.

Printed in the United States of America 1 2 3 4 5 6 7 8 9 10 99 98 97 96 95 94

ISBN: 0-835-91030-X

GLOBE FEARON
EDUCATIONAL PUBLISHER
PARAMUS, NEW JERSEY

Paramount Publishing

Contents

Appendix 307

A Note from the Publisher
to the Student

Do you look at the word *economics* and wonder what
such a difficult and serious-sounding word could
possibly have to do with you?

Believe it or not, economics is part of your everyday
life. Did you ever wonder why some people have jobs
and some people don't? And why is it that prices
sometimes go up, and sometimes go down? Why are
there sometimes shortages of things such as gasoline?
Why are some people rich and some people poor?
Why are some *countries* rich and some poor? The
study of economics can give you answers to these
questions as well as many others.

Economics is all about making choices. Suppose your
state government decides to spend less money on
schools and more money on roads this year. This is
an economic choice. Suppose your family decides to
fix up the old car instead of shopping for another one.
That is an economic choice. Or suppose you splurge
a little and take a friend to lunch today. Even that is
an economic choice.

Making wise economic choices is a skill—one that
both governments and individuals need in order to
be successful. This book looks at the principles of
economics and how they work. Knowledge of these
principles will help you understand many events in the
news and your responsibility as a citizen. How you use
these principles to make choices will affect how you
live now and in the future.

Every chapter in this book applies economic principles
to situations and experiences that may already be
familiar to you. You can add meaning to what you

read by asking certain questions as you go along. For example: *How can this information help me start a successful business? How can it help me get the right job? What examples of this economic principle in action can I find in the news or even in my own neighborhood? How can I use this information to better manage my time, money, and energy?* By thinking through the answers to such questions, you will find that economics has many practical applications that are useful to you.

Look for the notes in the margins of the pages. These notes provide interesting facts and thoughtful questions. Sometimes they give examples, and sometimes they help you review things you have already read about.

Other study aids are provided in each chapter. Read the **Chapter Learning Objectives** to help you focus on what you are about to learn. The list of **Words to Know** will help you become familiar with difficult vocabulary words that you'll find in your reading. **Economics Practice** questions will help you review and remember key points in each of the chapters. The **Chapter Summary** will help you prepare for the final **Chapter Quiz**.

We hope you enjoy this introduction to the fascinating field of economics. Everyone who worked on this book did their best to make it understandable, interesting, and useful. The rest is up to you. We wish you well in your studies. Our success is in your accomplishment.

Carol Hegarty
Publisher

Introduction to Economics

Chapter 1
What Is Economics?

Economics is all about making choices such as, how we earn our money and how we spend it. What does economics have to do with this football game?

Chapter Learning Objectives
- Explain the meaning of economics.
- List the four factors of production.
- Give two examples of opportunity costs.
- Explain specialization.
- Name three things that influence productivity.

Words to Know

capital   human-made things, such as machines and tools, that are used to produce goods and services

economics   the study of how people, businesses, and governments choose to use their limited resources

entrepreneurs   people who come up with the ideas for producing goods and services. They are willing to take the risks of going into business.

factors of production   the four things needed to produce goods and services: natural resources, labor, capital, and entrepreneurs

goods   things that can be seen, touched, and bought or sold

labor   workers

natural resources   things provided by nature, such as wood, oil, and coal, that can be used to produce goods and services

opportunity cost   whatever is given up when a choice must be made; a trade-off

productivity   the amount of goods and services produced by a worker or business in a given time period

scarcity   not enough of a certain resource to satisfy people's needs and wants

service   an activity performed for others for money, such as teaching or selling

specialization   the use of resources to produce only a single or a few kinds of goods or services

technology   the use of science to create new or better goods and services or more efficient methods of production

Six-year-old Robert has a dollar in his hand. He received the dollar for doing small chores around the house. He can spend it as he chooses.

Robert decides he might like to buy a new toy. On the other hand, he'd love to spend the whole dollar on candy. But having money in his pocket also makes him feel good. So part of him wants to tuck the dollar away and save it. He is torn about what to do.

What would you rather
do with your money—
spend it or save it?
Why?

This young child faces the basic economic problem. It is the same economic problem that you deal with every day, whether you know it or not. This problem is faced by governments, businesses—in fact, by every organization and living person. It is the problem of **scarcity**: When you only have so much of something, how do you best use it?

Young Robert has many possible uses for his dollar. He could use the dollar to take care of his hunger. Or he could take care of his desire to play, or his desire to feel "rich." He has to make a choice. Even if he had millions of dollars, he would still have to make choices. There would still be limits to how much he could spend. In this world, no one will ever have the luxury of not having to choose. Economic decisions are a fact of life.

Why do you think even
a rich person has to
make choices about
how to spend money?

Economics is the study of how people, businesses, and nations make choices. It is the study of how we deal with scarcity, or how we use our limited resources. *Resources* are those things that can be used to produce goods and services.

Wants, Needs, Goods, and Services

What do you consider
to be your own basic
personal needs?

Needs are those things that everyone must have to survive. Food, clothing, and shelter are examples of basic personal needs.

Wants are the things people desire. Radios, TVs, cars, computers, and telephones may seem like basic needs in this world. But people survived long before these inventions. What do you think would happen if a great disaster wiped out all the electronics on earth? People might still be able to find ways to eat, drink, and live.

Like young Robert, people are always looking for ways to meet their needs and wants. To do this, they produce and buy goods and services. **Goods** are things you can see, touch, and buy or sell. Sunglasses, popcorn, and compact discs are examples of goods. A **service** is any work that a person does for others for money. The person who sells you popcorn when you're at the movies is performing a service. Doctors, lawyers, teachers, and professional athletes perform services, too.

Name three goods you have bought in the past year.

Name any goods or services you can find in this picture.

Economics Practice

Write answers to the following questions on a separate sheet of paper.

1. When was the last time you bought or sold goods? What did you buy or sell?

2. What is the last service you bought or performed?

3. When you last bought a good or service, were you meeting a need or a want? Explain.

The Four Factors of Production

Long ago, a cave dweller chipped a tool out of stone. This early human used resources to produce a good. The resources used included the stone, another stone used as a chipping tool, work, and ideas.

All goods and services are produced with limited economic resources. These resources are called the **factors of production.** They can be put into four important groups: *natural resources, capital, labor,* and *entrepreneurs.*

Natural resources include sunlight, water, air, land, animals, fish, coal, oil, and so forth. Most of them, with the exception of resources such as sunlight, are only available in limited amounts. These resources are extremely important. Without them, our basic needs and wants could never be met. They are used to produce all kinds of goods and services.

Labor is another word for workers, or *human resources.* Workers are the people who produce goods and services. The factory worker, the computer operator, and the fast-food salesperson are examples of labor resources.

In economics, *capital* refers to capital goods. But *capital* can also mean wealth, such as money or property, that is used to produce more wealth.

Capital includes things, such as machines and tools, that are used to produce goods and services. Suppose you wanted to start a band. Your instruments and sound equipment are your capital. Without them, you could not produce your music.

Entrepreneurs are people with ideas for creating new goods and services. They are willing to take the risks of going into business. In 1869, an entrepreneur took the risk of starting the first professional baseball team—the Cincinnati Red Stockings. At the end of the 19th century, entrepreneurs raced to put together an efficient automobile engine. And today, entrepreneurs risk money and time to have medicines developed.

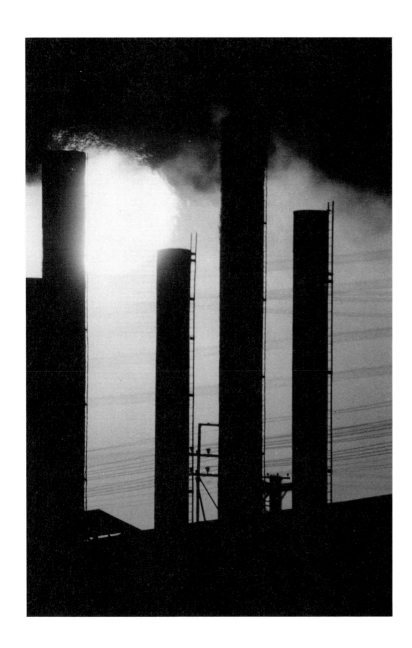

Do you think there can ever be a scarcity of clean air? Why or why not?

How is going into business for yourself different from working for another person? What kinds of risks must you take?

These medicines may someday cure diseases such as cancer and AIDS. Without entrepreneurs and their ideas, there would be far fewer new or improved goods and services.

Economics Practice

Write answers to the following questions on a separate sheet of paper.

1. A book is a good that is produced with each of the four factors of production. These include paper made from wood (natural resource); writer (labor); printing machines (capital); and publisher (entrepreneur). Give another example of a good, and list the four factors of production used to produce it.

2. Explain the differences between "labor" and "entrepreneur." Why are both important for producing goods and services?

Opportunity Costs

Because of scarcity, people have to make choices. Think about John. His uncle has offered him a good, full-time job in an auto body shop. He'll make $20 an hour as soon as he graduates from high school. But he's always had a dream of becoming a TV news reporter. To get this job, he will need to take certain classes at his local college. But the classes are only offered in the daytime. If he chooses to go to school, he'll have to turn down the job with his uncle. There is a trade-off involved.

John has to make a choice about how he will use his limited time and energy. John is looking at the *cost* of making one choice over another. If he takes the job, he can probably get an apartment and buy a nice car right away. But it will cost him the opportunity of becoming a TV news reporter. If he goes to school, he has a chance of becoming a reporter. But the cost will be giving up his good salary at the auto body shop. And he will also have to give up all the great things he wants to buy right away.

Whatever is given up when a choice is made is an **opportunity cost**. Opportunity costs occur any time a choice is made. When a business decides to produce cars instead of trucks, the opportunity cost is trucks. What happens when a government cuts welfare spending instead of the defense budget? The opportunity cost is aid for the poor.

The next time you have to make a decision, look at your top two choices. The thing that you will have to give up is the opportunity cost.

Economics Practice

Write answers to the following questions on a separate sheet of paper.

1. Suppose you were John. What choice would you make? What would be the opportunity cost?

2. When young people drop out of high school, what is the opportunity cost?

3. Describe the last time you had to make a choice. What was the opportunity cost?

Specialization

Drive across the plains of Iowa in late summer. You'll see miles and miles of corn blowing in the wind. If Iowa's farmers tried to grow coffee, peanuts, and bananas as well, they'd be sorry. Iowa has the perfect land and climate for growing corn but not for growing these other crops. The farmers are better off specializing in corn. That way, they make the most of Iowa's natural resources.

Corn growing in Iowa. What does it take to specialize in this product?

The economic idea of **specialization** helps them do this. You specialize as a student. This lets you dedicate your time and energy to learning. Most people tend to specialize in what they are best at. When people specialize, they are more productive than if each person were to do many different jobs. Businesses often specialize in producing one type of good or service. In this way, they can use capital and labor efficiently. Huge governments are broken into smaller departments and bureaus. Each specializes in handling certain services and problems for taxpayers.

If you could specialize in anything you wanted to, what would it be?

Productivity

Productivity is the amount of goods and services produced by a worker or business in a given time period. For example, Ed can catch five fish in an hour. But Ted can catch 25 fish in an hour. So Ted is more productive than Ed.

You've just read how specialization can lead to greater productivity. Capital, education, and technology also play an important role in productivity. For example, think about that Iowa farmer planting his crops. Picture him working in his fields with an old plow pulled by horses. Now imagine him driving across the fields on a brand new tractor. In each case, he is using different equipment (one type of capital) to produce his crop. Which do you think will lead to greater productivity?

Education also has a powerful effect on productivity. American businesses worry that many people are not prepared to work in today's workplace. Today's workers need strong reading, math, and problem-solving skills to understand electronics and operate complicated machinery. Education can also be linked to better ideas that improve productivity. People who can think creatively can help a workplace become more productive. They can find more effective ways to manage people and to use limited resources.

Technology has given us the atomic bomb. Do you think the world would have been better off without this weapon?

Finally, technology is important for productivity. **Technology** is science at work. New technology allows us to produce new or better products and services. Technology has given the world computers, robots, and video. It has changed the way people work and play. Twenty years ago, you would not have seen computers in a high school classroom. Cable TV was unheard of. Electronic cash registers were not used in stores. Technology has enabled us to work more quickly and keep better records than ever before.

Economics Practice

Write answers to the following questions on a separate sheet of paper.

1. Name a business in your city. What does the business specialize in?

2. Do you think education is important in the United States? Give two reasons why or why not.

3. Give one example of how technology has helped you to be more productive.

Economic Decision Making: High-Definition TV

Imagine a TV screen six feet wide with a picture four times sharper than today's average TV. It's more lifelike than anything you've ever seen before. This product of the near future is called high-definition TV (HDTV). It uses new technology currently being developed in Japan, the United States, and Europe.

Every evening some 94.9 million Americans tune in to prime-time TV. American companies know there's a lot of money to be made selling and servicing high-definition TVs. But they also know they face a great challenge in trying to compete with

Japanese technology. Some American companies have asked the government for millions of dollars to help with research and development *(R and D)*.

Should our government support this kind of research with tax dollars? Or should the companies spend their own dollars for technology research? What do you think?

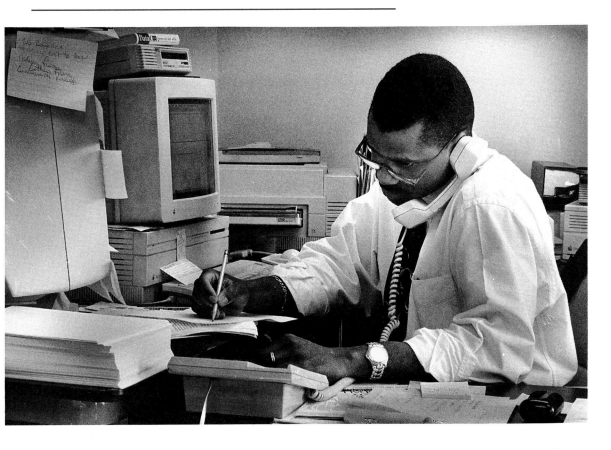

Thanks to technology, many jobs can be done more accurately and quickly.

Chapter Review

Chapter Summary

- Economics is the study of how people, businesses, and nations use their scarce or limited resources.

- Goods and services are produced to satisfy people's needs and wants.

- The four factors of production are natural resources, capital, labor, and entrepreneurs.

- Whenever an economic choice is made, a trade-off occurs. Whatever is given up is called the opportunity cost.

- Specialization is the use of resources to produce only a single or a few kinds of goods or services.

- People tend to specialize in what they do best. This leads to greater productivity.

- Capital, education, and technology also play a role in productivity.

Chapter Quiz

Write answers to the following questions on a separate sheet of paper.

A. Thinking About Economics

1. What is economics?

2. List the four factors of production.

3. Name five natural resources.

4. Give an example of a good that fills an economic need. Explain.

5. Give an example of a service that fills an economic want. Explain.

6. How are workers and entrepreneurs the same? How are they different?

7. A man can spend his $7 to go to the movies or to the ball game. He chooses to go to the movies. What is the opportunity cost?

8. Why do people specialize?

9. Name three things besides specialization that play a role in productivity.

10. Give an example of how technology can help people to be more productive.

B. Personal Economics

Give an example of an economic decision you had to make. What was the opportunity cost?

C. World Economics

In 1990, the United Nations held a World Summit for Children. There, world leaders discussed how resources could best be used to meet the needs of children. What resources do you think they might have been talking about? What would you consider to be the most important needs of the world's children?

Chapter 2

Economic Systems

In traditional economic systems, past ways of life determine how goods and services are produced and distributed.

Chapter Learning Objectives

- List the three basic questions that economic systems answer.
- Compare and contrast *traditional, command,* and *market* economic systems.
- Describe a mixed economic system.
- Outline the goals of most economic systems.

Words to Know

command system an economic system in which the government controls the production and distribution of goods and services

consumer a person who buys goods and services

economic system the way that a country or culture produces and distributes goods and services

market system an economic system in which individuals, not the government, control production and distribution of goods and services; also called *capitalism*

mixed system an economic system that includes both private ownership of property and government control of some services and industries

profit the money made by a business after all costs have been paid

standard of living a way to measure how well the needs and wants of citizens are being met by a country's economic system

traditional system an economic system based on past ways of life and culture

---

Mary Smith lives in Syracuse, New York. She stops at the supermarket on her way home from work. She rushes through the store past hundreds of different products. There are canned meats, paper towels, shampoo, microwave rice, milk, frozen pies, cat food, and motor oil. And although it is the dead of winter, there are many fresh fuits and vegetables as well. To Mary, the supermarket does not seem "super." She is used to having hundreds of different products to choose from.

Felicia Gomez lives in Oaxaca, Mexico. Every day she goes to the farmer's market to buy food for dinner. Farmers sit in stalls and sell their chickens, pigs, cheeses, and whatever fruits and vegetables are in season. It is rare to find canned, boxed, or frozen products here. Felicia always bargains with the shopkeepers for lower prices. They would not respect her if she didn't.

Do you think most Americans take their many choices for granted?

How can people in neighboring countries have such different experiences? Part of the answer lies in the country's economic system. An **economic system** is the way a government tries to satisfy its people's needs and wants. Economic systems answer these three basic questions:

1. What goods and services should be produced?
2. How should those goods and services be produced?
3. Who should get the goods and services?

There are three basic types of economic systems. They are the *traditional, command,* and *market systems.* Each system answers these questions differently.

The Traditional Economic System

Before Europeans arrived, the Australian aborigines lived very simple lives. They did not particularly care about gaining great personal wealth. They produced and traded goods and services—food, shelter, boomerangs for hunting—to satisfy their basic needs. Young men became hunters. Young women gathered food and took care of their families. Land belonging to the tribe was passed down from one generation to the next. Other kinds of personal property meant little to the aborigines. People willingly shared and traded basic goods and services.

The aborigines lived in a traditional economic system. In a **traditional system**, past beliefs and ways of doing things determine what goods and services should be produced. Tradition also determines how the goods and services should be produced, and who should get them. Such traditional economic systems can still be found today. They exist among the Ainu of Japan, the native people of Brazil's rainforest, and the Amish in the United States. In such cultures, young men follow in their fathers' footsteps. Young women take on their mothers' roles. Leaders govern by laws and practices that have been in place for many years.

Economics Practice

Write answers to the following questions on a separate sheet of paper.

1. In the Australian aborigine culture, what goods and services were produced?

2. How were goods and services distributed?

3. Does the aborigines' economic system appeal to you? Give two reasons why or why not.

The Market Economic System

In a pure **market system**, individuals are powerful. The government has little or no say in answering the three basic economic questions. Buyers and sellers make the economic decisions. The market economic system is also called *capitalism*.

Here's how it works. In a pure market system, Henry Chin decides to start a business which produces chocolate-covered peanuts. He covers some nuts in white chocolate and some in milk chocolate. He then sells them by mail order and in grocery stores. He is free to produce and sell these nuts any way he wants to. That is, as long as he doesn't break any laws.

Buyers in a market system have the freedom to buy the nuts or not to buy them. Their decisions will determine whether or not Henry Chin keeps producing the chocolate nuts. Their decisions will also determine how many nuts get produced and what their price will be. In this way, the economic questions of *what*, *how*, and *for whom* are answered in the marketplace.

The United States comes close to having a pure market economic system. Think about your own power as an individual in the system. You can start your own business if you have the resources. You can buy what you want and sell what you want. The goods and services you see on the market are based on **consumer** buying decisions. Businesses produce what consumers need and want.

> The market economy in the United States is often called the *free-enterprise* system. "Enterprise" means business.

Economics Practice

Write answers to the following questions on a separate sheet of paper.

1. Suppose millions of American consumers suddenly stopped buying hamburgers and started eating tofu instead. What would happen to jobs at Burger King or McDonald's? What would happen to jobs at vegetarian restaurants?

2. What resources does Henry Chin need to produce chocolate-covered nuts? List at least four.

The Characteristics of a Market Economy

The United States is not a pure market economy. The government does have some say in how goods and services are produced. For example, there are consumer laws that regulate safety features in cars. Pollution control standards regulate the kind of waste that factories can produce. Minimum wage laws set wages for some workers. And equal opportunity laws say that sellers must not discriminate based on sex, religion, race, or age when they hire workers. But for the most part, the United States is a market economy. Market economies have these characteristics:

1. *People are free to own property.* Everyone has the right to own their own homes, cars, and businesses. The government cannot take away that right.

2. *Most businesses are owned by individuals.* In the United States, for example, most stores and services are privately owned. The government even buys weapons from private business. Government services such as postal delivery and low-income housing are exceptions to this rule.

3. *People are free to run any type of business within the law.* Remember Henry Chin? In the United States, the government allows him to produce the chocolate-covered nuts. He can do whatever he likes as long as he has the resources and stays within the law.

4. *People have economic freedom of choice.* They can choose the kinds of jobs they want, what to buy, and what to sell.

5. *People are free to compete.* If there is only one gas station in town, you are free to open another one. The owner of the first gas station may not like the competition. But he has no power to stop you.

6. *Businesses are allowed to make and keep their profits.* A **profit** is the money left over after production and selling costs have been paid. Most people in the United States start their own businesses because they want to make a profit. The more profit they make, the better life they believe they can have.

In the United States, business and government are not totally separate. For example, a government law requires many private businesses to meet access requirements for handicapped citizens.

How would you feel if someone else could tell you what job you could or could not do?

Economics Practice

Write answers to the following questions on a separate sheet of paper.

1. Is making a profit important to you? Explain.

2. Name three competing businesses in your city.

3. Does your school operate to make a profit? Explain.

The Command Economic System

Imagine that you work in a factory. For years you have been producing tractors. One day the manager of the plant calls a meeting. "We won't be producing tractors any longer," she says. "The government wants us to begin producing heavy-duty trucks. We'll be making this change over the next several months."

In a pure **command system**, the government could control the economy in this way. The government could be run by one person or group of leaders. They decide what goods and services should be produced. They choose what food is farmed, what machines are made, and how they are used. Available jobs are based on the government's decisions. The government also decides how the goods are distributed. Perhaps a small group of citizens would become wealthy while most stayed poor. Or perhaps all goods and services would be available equally to all people.

Up until recently, Russia had a command economic system. Russia was part of the Soviet Union. For the most part, the government controlled production of all goods and services. Government planning agencies decided what would be made and how. All products and services—from TVs to refrigerators—were distributed by government planners. And the government set prices on most goods and services as well.

The Soviet Union's command system was set up after the Communist Revolution in 1917. The Russian Communists took their ideas from Karl Marx. The command system did not work well in the Soviet Union. There were great shortages of many goods and services. People had to wait in long lines to buy things.

On August 1991, there was another revolution. This led to the break up of the Soviet Union into fifteen separate republics. Russia is one of these countries. The Russian government has tried to change Russia to make it more like a free market economy. Some businesses once run by the government have been sold to the people. The new business owners can try to make profits.

Changing the Soviet Union from a command system to a market economy is not easy. Many people are still suffering. But many Russians see that the market system is successful in other countries. They hope they will soon enjoy a similar success.

Great Economic Thinkers: Karl Marx

Karl Marx was born in Germany in 1818. But he lived most of his life in England, where he died in 1883. He wrote many books and papers. In them he predicted what he thought would happen because of struggles between the rich and the poor.

Marx believed economic systems would go through different stages. He thought capitalism, with private ownership of the factors of production, was doomed to fail. This was because Marx thought poor workers were unfairly taken advantage of by wealthy capitalists. He said that eventually the working class would unite and revolt against the capitalists. This would be called a "Communist Revolution."

Next would come a temporary period called *socialism*. Today socialism usually means government control of major industries. To Marx, the workers would control *all* production under socialism. Eventually all private property would be done away with. There would no longer be classes of rich people and poor. Then communism would exist.

Under Marxist communism, the factors of production would be owned by everyone together. People would produce according to their abilities. And goods and services would be distributed according to people's needs.

Marx's predictions about the failure of capitalism have not taken place. Instead, under capitalist systems, working conditions and workers' wages have greatly improved since Marx's time. There have been none of the true workers' revolutions which Marx predicted. Even so, Marx's ideas have been important in many countries and are important in the history of economic thought.

Karl Marx (1818–1883)

Mixed Economic Systems

All economic systems are a mix of traditional, market and command economies. In a **mixed system**, the government has a hand in providing goods and services and keeping the economy healthy. However, individuals can also own property and control some of the factors of production. The degree to which a system is mixed varies. You've already read how the United States is mainly a market system. And you know that it has some characteristics of a command economy as well. Another strong example of a mixed system can be found in the country of Sweden. The Swedish government owns means of transportation such as railroads and airlines. Also, health care is provided by the Swedish government. Yet there are also many Swedish businesses that are privately owned by individuals.

The Changing Economic World

The changes in the economic system in the former Soviet Union caused great unrest and upheaval in Eastern Europe. Many smaller countries formerly under Soviet economic control have become free. Czechoslovakia, Poland, Hungary, Romania, and Bulgaria all have new governments. These countries are in the process of setting up democracies and free market systems.

Another important change is the reunion of East and West Germany. Germany was split into two countries after World War II. East Germans had a command economic system. The West Germans have a strong mixed economic system. One of the challenges of reuniting this country is successfully joining the two economic systems.

Goals of Economic Systems

Imagine a country where everyone has enough to eat and a good place to live. Imagine a country where everyone who can work has a job. Imagine a place where all of the people have access to medical care.

Most countries believe these things can happen if there is a strong, efficient economy. They believe a healthy economy is a growing, secure one. In such an

**The Berlin Wall dividing East and West Germany
was torn down in 1990.**

economy, new and better goods and services are
constantly being produced in the best possible way.
Producing goods and services means jobs. Jobs mean
that people have the ability to buy goods and services
and pay taxes. And all this, in turn, leads again to more
and better goods and services.

Countries hope strong economies will produce a
high **standard of living** for their citizens. A country's
standard of living is one way to judge how well an
economy is doing. The standard of living considers
the availability and quality of food, shelter, education,
and health care. In general, the higher a population's
standard of living, the healthier the economy.

Chapter Review

Chapter Summary

- Economic systems answer the following questions: What should be produced, how should it be produced, and for whom should it be produced?

- The traditional economic system answers the three questions based on past beliefs, ways of life, and culture.

- In the market or capitalist economic system, individual buyers and sellers decide on production and prices.

- In a command economic system, one person or group of people controls production and distribution.

- In mixed economic systems, both individuals and the government make decisions about production. All economic systems are mixed to varying degrees.

- Most countries have the same economic goals: efficiency, growth, and security. They believe a strong, healthy economic system will bring about a high standard of living for citizens.

Chapter Quiz

Write answers to the following questions on a separate sheet of paper.

A. Thinking About Economics

1. What questions do economic systems answer?

2. How are these questions answered in a traditional economy?

3. Give one example of a traditional economy.

4. In a pure market economy, who controls production?

5. In a command market economy, who controls production?

6. Sweden has a mixed economic system. Give one example of how it is like a market system. Give one example of how it is like a command system.

7. What are three important characteristics of a market economy? Explain.

8. Is the United States economy a pure market economy? Explain.

9. What does a country's standard of living measure?

B. Personal Economics

What kinds of decisions do you make as a consumer in the market system of the United States? How can a business be affected by consumer decisions?

C. World Economics

In some countries, such as Russia, China, and Sweden, the government offers free health care to citizens. Do you think it is a government's responsibility to offer free health care? Or should health care be part of the market system? Give at least three reasons for your opinion.

Unit One Review

Write answers to the following questions on a separate sheet of paper.

1. What is economics?

2. What are the four factors of production?

3. What is the difference between economic needs and wants?

4. How does specialization lead to higher productivity?

5. What role does education play in increasing productivity?

6. What three questions do all economic systems answer?

7. In a market economy, who owns most of the businesses?

8. In a command economy, who controls most of the major businesses?

9. What is a mixed economic system?

10. What economic goals do most countries share?

The American Free Enterprise System

Chapter 3

Consumers and Demand

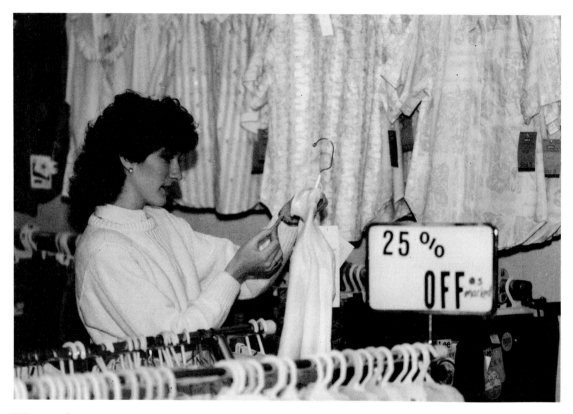

When prices come down, consumers are willing and able to buy more goods and services.

Chapter Learning Objectives

- Explain the law of demand.
- Use a graph to interpret a demand curve.
- List four things that can affect consumer demand.
- Explain how demand will increase or decrease under certain conditions.

Words to Know

complementary goods   goods that are used with each other, such as cars and tires

demand   the amount of a good or service that consumers are willing and able to buy at different prices

demand curve   the line on a graph that represents the amount of a good or service that consumers will buy at different prices

graph   a diagram that shows the relationship between two or more sets of things

income   the amount of money that a person makes in a certain period of time

interchangeable   capable of being put in place of one another

law of demand   the economic law which states that consumers will buy more of a good or service as the price goes down

substitute goods   goods that can take the place of one another

---

It is the Saturday after Christmas—one of the biggest shopping days of the year. A crowd has been waiting outside of Hewlett's Department Store since 7:00 A.M. Some people have brought coffee and rolls from home. Others lean against the cold, brick wall of the store and catch up on their sleep. Still others scan the newspaper ads for bargains and sales: "Prices slashed," "40%—50%—even 60% off storewide," "Biggest bargains of the year." The customers make lists of what they will buy.

When the doors open, the crowd streams in. The people buy large amounts of clothing, holiday decorations, cookware, and jewelry. A TV crew comes to cover the action.

"Excuse me," says the reporter to a consumer leaving the store. "What did you buy?"

"I bought seven boxes of Christmas cards, three sets of bed sheets, and six turtleneck sweaters."

"Why so much?" asks the reporter. "What are you going to do with all of it?"

"Some I'll use now, some I'll save until next year. Heck, at these prices, I'll buy whatever they want to sell me."

The Law of Demand

Suppose you are explaining the law of demand to a friend. She asks you when Congress passed this law. What would you say?

This story gives a good example of the economic law of demand. **Demand** is the amount of a good or service that consumers are willing and able to buy at different prices. The **law of demand** states that consumers will usually be willing and able to buy more of a good or service as the price goes down. Store owners know this. If they want to sell something in a hurry, they lower the price. In the United States market economy, demand is very important. As you will see in this unit, it is one of the forces that helps determine the price of goods and services.

Here's another example to illustrate demand. Cal, an artistic high school student, makes and sells hand-painted T-shirts to students. He calls his shirts "Cal's Custom T's." He sells them to the students in his high school. At $10 each, the high school consumers as a group will buy 45 T-shirts a semester. At $20 each, they are willing and able to buy 30. At $40, no one is willing and able to buy the shirts, so there is no demand. The words *willing* and *able* are important here. Cal's Custom T's are *not* in demand if students want them but cannot pay for them. They are only in demand when students want them *and* have the money to pay for them.

Another way to look at demand is on a **graph.** Graph 3.1 is a line graph. It shows the demand for Cal's Custom T's. The vertical axis (on the far left) shows different prices of T-shirts. The horizontal axis (along the bottom) shows different amounts of T-shirts bought.

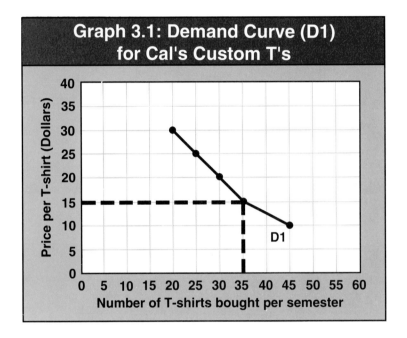

Graph 3.1: Demand Curve (D1) for Cal's Custom T's

On Graph 3.1, you can see how demand works. For example, at $15 each, students are willing and able to buy 35 T-shirts. The line on the graph is called a **demand curve** (D1). It gives you a good picture of the law of demand. As prices go down, people are willing and able to buy more.

What is a good or service that is in high demand among your friends?

Economics Practice

Write answers to the following questions on a separate sheet of paper.

1. Look at Graph 3.1. What is the amount demanded for Cal's Custom T's at $25 each?

2. According to Graph 3.1, are people willing and able to buy more T-shirts or fewer as the price goes down? What happens when the price goes up?

3. Imagine a beautiful sports car that sells for $125,000. Millions of people would love to buy it. But only a few people can afford it. Do you think people would buy more cars or fewer if the price of the sports car somehow came down to $25,000? Explain.

What Can Change Demand?

The demand curve shows the amount of a good or service that consumers are willing and able to buy at different prices. Demand can be affected by things other than price. For example, consumers' likes and dislikes can easily increase or decrease demand for an item. Clothing styles are entirely different now than they were 100 years ago. Why? Partly because tastes change. If there is any demand at all now for women's corsets (very tight girdles) and sun bonnets, it is very low. But at the turn of the century, these were popular items in high demand.

An increase or decrease in demand can be shown on a graph. Once again, look at the example of Cal's Custom T's. Suppose the casual look is in for fall. Demand for the T-shirts will probably increase. Graph 3.2 on page 38 shows the original demand curve as D1. The demand curve labeled D2 shows a shift to the *right*. This shift means that demand has increased. At each price, people will buy more.

Women's fashions at the turn of the century were quite different from today's styles.

Greater interest in casual style causes an increase in demand (D2).

Less interest in casual style causes a decrease in demand (D2).

Now suppose that in the fall the casual look had never become popular. Instead, people wanted to dress in a more formal style. Demand for Cal's Custom T's decreases. The demand curve labeled D2 shows a shift to the *left*. This means that at each price, people will buy less. See Graph 3.3.

Economics Practice

1. Originally, at $30 each, students would buy 20 T-shirts. Now that T-shirts are "in," how many will students buy at $30 each? Use the demand curve labeled D2 on Graph 3.2 to find the answer.

2. If T-shirts are no longer in fashion, how many will students buy at $30 each? Use the demand curve labeled D2 on Graph 3.3 to find the answer.

How Income and Substitute Goods Affect Demand

Demand is affected by likes and dislikes. Demand can also be affected by income. **Income** is the amount of money a person makes in a certain period of time. Suppose a large number of students got raises at their part-time jobs. They might be willing and able to use this income to buy more of Cal's Custom T's. This would mean an increase in demand. On the other hand, if students' incomes decreased, they might buy fewer of Cal's T-shirts. They couldn't afford as many.

Demand is also affected by the price of **substitute goods** or services. A substitute is a good or service that can take the place of another. For example, margarine can be substituted for butter. Powdered milk can take the place of fresh cow's milk. Hair styling gels can replace hairsprays, and so on.

If incomes increase and demand goes up for Cal's Custom T's, which way will the demand curve shift? Why?

What is a substitute good for ice cream? If the price of that good goes down, which way will the demand curve for ice cream shift?

Because these goods are **interchangeable,** the price of one substitute good will affect the demand for another. For example, suppose that there are some machine-made T-shirts that look almost as good as Cal's Custom T's. When the price of these machine-made T-shirts goes down, the demand for Cal's Custom T's decreases. Why? Consumers will usually go for the lower-priced good or service. Now suppose the price of the machine-made T-shirts goes up. Demand for Cal's Custom T's will increase. People will switch to buy the less expensive substitute.

Economics Practice

1. Suppose the price of butter goes up. Will the demand for margarine increase or decrease? Why?

2. Suppose the price of butter goes down. Will the demand for margarine increase or decrease? Why?

How Complementary Goods Affect Demand

What are two complementary goods that you use?

Complementary goods and services can also affect demand. **Complementary goods** and services are things that are often used together. For example, spaghetti is often used with tomato sauce. Peanut butter is often used with jelly. Cassette tapes and cassette recorders are always used together. These things complement each other.

The price of a good or service will often affect the demand for its complement. Suppose students always wear Cal's Custom T's with blue jeans. The blue jeans and T-shirts are complementary goods. If the price of blue jeans goes up, it is likely that the demand for T-shirts will go down. Why? The students can buy fewer blue jeans. It follows that they will want fewer T-shirts, since they won't have anything to wear with them. Now if the price of blue jeans goes down, the demand for T-shirts will go up. Why? The students will be able to buy more blue jeans. They will want more T-shirts to go with them.

Economics Practice

Write answers to the following questions on a separate sheet of paper.

1. Are CDs (compact discs) and tape cassettes substitute or complementary goods? Explain.

2. Suppose the price of CDs goes up. Will the demand for tape cassettes increase or decrease? Explain.

3. Are CDs and CD players substitute or complementary goods? Explain.

4. Suppose the price of CDs goes up. Will the demand for CD players increase or decrease? Explain.

William Stanley Jevons (1835–1882)

Great Economic Thinkers: W. S. Jevons

William Stanley Jevons was a British economist who lived from 1835 to 1882. One of his important thoughts was about why people buy more of a good or service when the price goes down. This was Jevons' idea: As people buy more and more of something, they get less and less satisfaction from the extra amounts. Therefore they will only buy more if the price goes down.

For example, let's say that you really like hot fudge sundaes. In fact, you like them so much that right now you'd pay $5 for a large sundae. So you go ahead and buy one that is smothered in fudge, with whipped cream and a cherry. After you eat one sundae, you're still hungry and would like more. But for the next one you're only willing to pay $2. That second sundae wouldn't give you as much satisfaction as the first. Your third hot fudge sundae gives you even less satisfaction than the second. So you're only willing to pay $1 for it. After three hot fudge sundaes, you've had more than enough. You're so full that you wouldn't pay any amount for a fourth.

Jevons' idea, as shown in the hot fudge sundae example, is called "the law of diminishing marginal utility." *Utility* means the satisfaction that people get from consuming something. In economics, *marginal* refers to the last unit of something produced or consumed. In this example, Jevons' law means that you get less satisfaction from each additional sundae you eat.

Jevons' idea explains the law of demand, which says that people buy more when prices go down. His thoughts caused other economists of his time to think more about demand.

Chapter Review

Chapter Summary

- Demand refers to the amount of a good or service that consumers are willing and able to pay at different prices.

- The law of demand states that consumers are willing and able to buy more of a good or service as the price goes down. This law is seen on a demand curve.

- When demand changes, more (or less) is bought at each price. When demand increases, a demand curve will shift to the right. When demand decreases, the demand curve will shift to the left.

- Demand can be affected by consumer tastes, incomes, and the price of complementary and substitute goods.

Chapter Quiz

Write answers to the following questions on a separate sheet of paper.

A. Thinking About Economics

1. What is the law of demand?

2. Give an example of complementary goods.

3. Suppose the price of one of your complementary goods from question 2 goes up. How will it affect demand for its partner?

4. Give an example of substitute goods.

5. Suppose the price of one of your substitute goods from question 4 goes down. How will it affect demand for its partner?

6. Suppose a group of consumers gets a pay raise. How might it affect the demand for steak among this group?

Graph 3.4: Demand Curve for Sally's Hamburgers

Price per hamburger (Dollars)

Number of hamburgers bought daily at Sally's Hamburgers

Use Graph 3.4 to answer the following questions.

7. At a price of $1 each, how many hamburgers will Sally's customers buy each day?

8. At a price of $10 each, how many hamburgers will Sally's customers buy each day?

9. Give one reason why this demand curve might shift to the right (why there might be an increase in demand).

10. Give one reason why this demand curve might shift to the left (why there might be a decrease in demand).

B. Personal Economics

Suppose you have $20, and you want to buy a sweater that costs $12.95.

a. What might be a good substitute for the sweater?

b. What products might be complements for the sweater?

c. What are some things you could do with your money other than buying the sweater?

d. If the price of the sweater went up to $20 (tax included), would this affect your buying decision? Explain.

e. If you got $30 from your aunt for your birthday, how would this affect your buying decision?

C. World Economics

Often consumers demand things that are produced in other countries. For example, consumers in Mexico buy computers produced in the United States. Consumers in the United States buy clothing produced in Mexico. Selling to other countries is an important part of demand for some goods.

a. Japanese restaurants start buying more beef from the United States. What would happen to the demand curve for U.S. beef? Explain.

b. If the price of rice imported from Japan increases, what would happen to the demand for rice grown in California? Explain.

Chapter 4

Producers and Supply

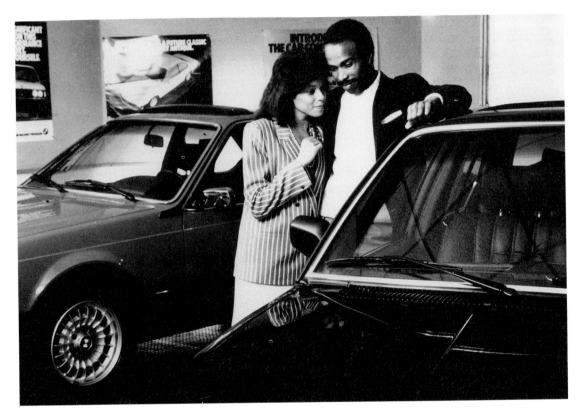

When the prices of new cars rise, producers will usually be willing and able to supply more cars for consumers.

Chapter Learning Objectives

- Explain the law of supply.
- Use a graph to interpret a supply curve.
- List three things that can affect supply.
- Explain how prices affect what producers are willing to supply.

Words to Know

cost of production   costs of things such as natural resources, capital, and labor, which must be paid by producers

executives   people responsible for directing and managing a business

incentives   things that encourage people to work harder or to produce more

law of supply   the economic law which states that producers are willing to supply more of a good or service as the price becomes higher

supply   the amount of a good or service that producers are willing and able to produce at different prices

supply curve the line on a graph that represents the amount of a good or service that producers are willing to supply at different prices

A group of automobile **executives** are holding a meeting. They have to decide on a manufacturing and sales plan for the coming year. They look over the company sales figures for the last year. They notice that all of their compact and mid-size cars have sold very well. In the middle of the year, they had raised the price of these cars by 5%. The cars had continued to sell just as well.

The executives decide that for the coming year they will produce 10% more cars than in the previous year. And if sales continue to do well, they will consider another price increase.

The Law of Supply

This story about the car-makers is an example of the law of supply. In the United States market economy, people want to make a profit. In Chapter 2, you read that profit is the money made by a business after all costs have been paid. When a business is successful, people earn profits in return for the risks of starting and running the business.

The **law of supply** states that when the price of a good or service rises, producers will usually be willing and able to supply more of that good or service. So higher prices are an **incentive** for producers to produce more. Supply, along with demand, helps set prices in a market economy.

In Chapter 3, you read about consumer demand for Cal's Custom T's. As the price for a T-shirt went down, people bought more T-shirts. The relationship between price and supply is just the opposite. At $10 each, Cal is only willing and able to supply ten T-shirts. Why? Because at $10 each, he doesn't stand to make much of a profit. He has to consider the cost of materials, the time he spends producing the T-shirts, and so forth. At a price much below $10 each, he will make no profit or take a loss.

On the other hand, at $20 each, he's willing and able to make 30 T-shirts. At $30, he'll gladly make 45. This will give Cal a good profit for the semester.

Graph 4.1 shows supply on a graph. Look at it now. The line on the graph is called a **supply curve** (S1).

On Graph 4.1, you can see how the law of supply works. For example, at $25 each, Cal is willing and able to produce 40 T-shirts. Like most producers, he is willing to produce more as prices get higher.

Economics Practice

Write answers to the following questions on a separate sheet of paper.

1. Look at Graph 4.1. How many shirts will Cal supply at $15 each?

2. Why do you think Cal would be more willing to supply more T-shirts at $30 each than at $10 each?

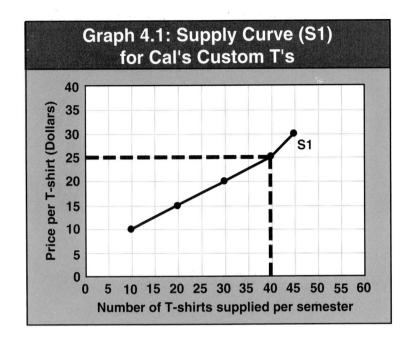

Graph 4.1: Supply Curve (S1) for Cal's Custom T's

Price per T-shirt (Dollars) / Number of T-shirts supplied per semester

What Can Change Supply?

In Chapter 3, you read about how the demand curve might shift with changes in things like tastes and incomes. Likewise, supply for a good or service can increase or decrease over time. By **supply**, we mean the amount of a good or service that producers are willing and able to produce at different prices.

One of the most important things affecting supply is the **cost of production.** Costs for things such as natural resources, capital, and labor must all be paid for by producers. When Cal produces his T-shirts, he buys white T-shirts and paint. He plans the design. Then he hand paints it. He must also deliver the shirt. He pays himself a salary for the work he does.

Suppose that suddenly the cost of white T-shirts goes up. Now at a price of $10, Cal is only willing to produce five T-shirts because his costs have gone up. On Graph 4.2 on page 50, this decrease is shown by a shift of the supply curve to the *left*.

A producer has to cover the cost of production. That's why higher prices are an incentive to produce more.

Suppose the cost of sugar goes up. How might the production of candy be affected?

Graph 4.2: Supply Curve (S1) with a Shift to the Left (S2)

Increased costs of production cause a decrease in supply (S2).

Economics Practice

Write answers to the following questions on a separate sheet of paper.

1. The supply curve labeled S1 shows what Cal was willing and able to supply before the rise in production costs. How many shirts would he produce at $30 each?

2. The supply curve labeled S2 shows what Cal was willing and able to supply after the rise in production costs. How many shirts would he now produce at $30 each?

How Technology Affects Supply

In Chapter 1, you read about how technology can help businesses produce more and better goods and services. In other words, technology can help to increase supply. Suppose a new paint is invented.

The paint is cheaper, more brilliant, dries faster, and is easier to work with. Cal finds he spends 40% less time on each T-shirt! He decides to supply more T-shirts at each price. This increase is shown on Graph 4.3 by a shift of the supply curve to the right.

Graph 4.3: Supply Curve (S1) with a Shift to the Right (S2)

Better technology causes an increase in supply (S2).

Economics Practice

Write answers to the following questions on a separate sheet of paper.

1. Originally, at $10 each, Cal would supply 10 T-shirts. Now that technology has helped him cut his costs, how many will he make at that price? Use the supply curve labeled S2 on Graph 4.3 to find the answer.

2. What other changes in technology might increase Cal's production?

Opportunity Costs Can Affect Supply, Too

Another thing that may affect supply is opportunity cost. Suppose that Cal discovers he can make more of a profit by making custom hats. He might choose to decrease the supply of T-shirts. Then he will use his resources to start making custom hats. Eventually, he will phase out his T-shirt business altogether. Cal is a pretty good business person. He knows that he has to keep pace with consumers' changing tastes!

For a business to be successful, producers must look carefully at production costs, available technology, and other ways to guarantee profits. All these things will figure into the amounts and kinds of goods and services that are supplied in a market economy.

Economic Decision Making: Labor Supply

Labor supply often works in much the same way as supply of a product such as Cal's Custom T's. For example, Bettina Bachmann is a foreign exchange student in the United States. She has come from Germany to study at a large university. To support herself, she translates English papers and video scripts into German.

At first, Bettina charged $15 an hour, a low rate for her services. "I was unsure of myself. I needed the experience. I was willing to make a smaller profit just to get started," says Bettina.

Why do you think Bettina is willing to work more hours at $30 an hour than at $15 an hour?

But as Bettina improved in her work skills, she decided she charged too little. "The costs started to outweigh the benefits. After all, I was taking time away from my studies. I decided I had to charge more to make it worth my while. Now I ask for $30 an hour. I usually get it. I am willing to work more hours. There seems to be a great demand for my services."

Chapter Review

Chapter Summary

- Supply is the amount of a good or service that producers are willing and able to produce at different prices.

- The law of supply states that producers are usually willing and able to produce more of a good or service as the price goes up. This law can easily be seen on a typical supply curve.

- When there is an increase in supply, the supply curve will shift to the right. When there is a decrease in supply, the supply curve will shift to the left.

- Supply can be affected by the cost of production, technology, and opportunity costs.

Chapter Quiz

Write answers to the following questions on a separate sheet of paper.

A. Thinking About Economics

1. What is the law of supply?

2. Why might a producer be willing to supply more of a good or service as the price becomes higher?

3. What are production costs?

4. List three production costs that might go into the production of cookies.

5. Suppose that the cost of flour used in making cookies suddenly goes up. How might that affect the supply of cookies?

6. Suppose that there is a new invention. It enables the cookie maker to bake cookies in half the normal time. How might that affect supply?

Graph 4.4: Supply Curve for Sally's Hamburgers

Price per hamburger (Dollars)

Number of hamburgers Sally will supply per day

Use Graph 4.4 to answer the following questions.

7. At a price of $1 each, how many hamburgers will Sally supply each day?

8. At a price of $10 each, how many hamburgers will Sally supply each day?

9. Give one reason why this supply curve might shift to the right (why there might be an increase in supply).

10. Give one reason why this supply curve might shift to the left (why there might be a decrease in supply).

B. Personal Economics

Suppose you owned a furniture company. You like what you do. But to make the kind of profit you want, you must work 65 to 80 hours per week. You're able to drive nice cars and own your own home. But there doesn't seem to be any time to have fun. What do you think would happen to your profit if you were willing to supply only 40 hours of work per week? What might happen to your business?

C. World Economics

Very few countries are able to produce all the goods and services they need and want. Most countries trade with other countries to get some of the things they want. For example, only a few countries in the world can supply diamonds. South Africa is the world's largest producer of diamonds. What do you think happens to the amount of diamonds South Africa is willing to supply when the price of diamonds goes up? What happens when the price of diamonds goes down?

Chapter 5
How Prices Are Determined

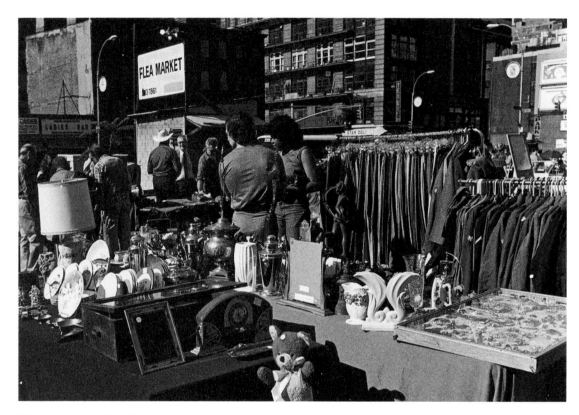

Many people like to shop at flea markets, where they can bargain for items. How do you think the buyers and sellers agree on prices?

Chapter Learning Objectives
- Explain how supply and demand together determine prices.
- Find how prices are set by using the supply and demand curves together.
- Describe a surplus, and explain how it is caused.
- Describe a shortage, and explain how it is caused.

Words to Know

equilibrium price   the price at which the amount demanded equals the amount supplied

intersect   to cross at a point. The point on a graph where a supply curve and a demand curve *intersect* marks the equilibrium price.

inventory   products that a business has in stock and that are ready to be sold

shortage   what happens when, at a given price, people want to buy more of a good or service than is available

surplus   what happens when, at a given price, more of a good or service is available than people want to buy

---

Theo is visiting the city flea market. This is the first time he has been there. He is amazed by the great variety of items that are being offered for sale.

Theo wanders down one row after another. He stops to look through a collection of used books that a young woman is selling. Then he admires a collection of oriental rugs.

It's a beautiful spring day, so Theo is in no hurry. He examines a display of old radios. Then he looks through a collection of record albums. Then he tries on two shirts and a sweater. The prices on all of these items seem OK to Theo. But he hasn't been able to make up his mind about what he really wants to buy.

Finally, Theo finds a used, portable color TV. The price on it is $100.

"I'd like this TV," he says to the old man selling it. "But I won't pay $100 for it. I'll give you $50."

"Forget it," says the old man. "I put $40 in new parts into it. That's not even counting my labor. No way will I sell it for $50."

"Well, OK, I'll give you $60," says Theo.

"Make it $75."

"I've got $70 in my pocket. It's all I have."

"Deal."

Who Sets Prices?

Theo and the old man have just shown you one way that prices are set in a market economy. Theo, the consumer, is willing and able to pay $70 for the set, but no more. The old man, the seller, is willing and able to sell the set for $70, but no less. Through supply and demand, the market price has been set at $70. The buyer and seller have agreed on the price.

Are you a consumer, a producer, or both?

These forces of supply and demand work together to determine prices every day. The prices you pay for food, housing, and entertainment are decided by consumers and producers, buyers and sellers. It is rare that the government has anything to do with setting prices in the American economy. In a free market economy, that job is usually left to businesses and buyers.

Supply and Demand on a Graph

In Chapters 3 and 4, you learned how supply and demand curves appear on a graph. As prices become lower, the amount buyers demand goes up. As prices get higher, the amount businesses supply goes up. Supply and demand curves work in opposite directions.

Graph 5.1: Supply (S) and Demand (D) Curves for Cal's Custom T's

Price per T-shirt (Dollars)

Number of T-shirts bought and sold per semester

If this is the case, how do prices ever get set? Take a look at Graph 5.1. It shows the supply and demand curves for Cal's Custom T's. The point where the two curves **intersect** or cross is the **equilibrium price**. It is the only point where consumers and producers agree on the price and the amount. At this price everything for sale should be sold, and nothing should be left.

On this graph, you can see the price for Cal's T-shirts. He will sell his shirts for $20 each to consumers. At this price, he will sell 30 shirts per semester. He is satisfied with his profit. And consumers are satisified with the price of the shirts.

This graph does not mean that Cal will *always* sell his shirts for $20. Remember, there are many forces that affect supply and demand. Incomes, consumer tastes, technology, and production costs change over time. As supply and demand change, prices change. These are constant forces at work in the economy.

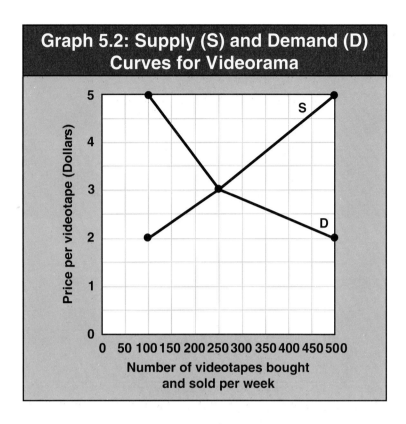

Graph 5.2: Supply (S) and Demand (D) Curves for Videorama

Economics Practice

Use Graph 5.2 to answer the following questions. Write your answers on a separate sheet of paper.

1. What is the equilibrium price of videotapes at Videorama?

2. At this price, how many videotapes will the consumers buy?

3. How many videotapes will Videorama sell?

What Happens When Prices Are Above the Equilibrium Price?

If sellers try to sell their goods for more than the equilibrium price, there will not be enough buyers. When this happens, there is a surplus of goods or services. A **surplus** means there are more goods available than consumers will buy at that price.

Suppose Cal had produced 45 T-shirts. He decides to ask $30 each for them. At this price, he can only sell 20 shirts. He will have a surplus of 25 left-over shirts. He will probably lower the price of his T-shirts in order to sell the extras.

When stores have sales, they are often trying to reduce their **inventory**. They want to get rid of their surplus goods. Graph 5.3 shows a supply curve and a demand curve for Cal's Custom T's. At prices above $20, the equilibrium price, surpluses exist.

Why would a store want to get rid of surplus goods?

What causes stores to have too much inventory?

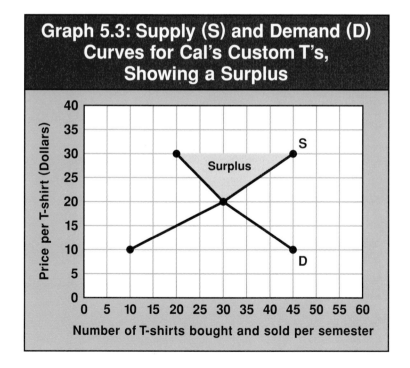

Graph 5.3: Supply (S) and Demand (D) Curves for Cal's Custom T's, Showing a Surplus

Price per T-shirt (Dollars)

Surplus

S

D

Number of T-shirts bought and sold per semester

At prices above $20 per T-shirt, the equilibrium price, surpluses exist.

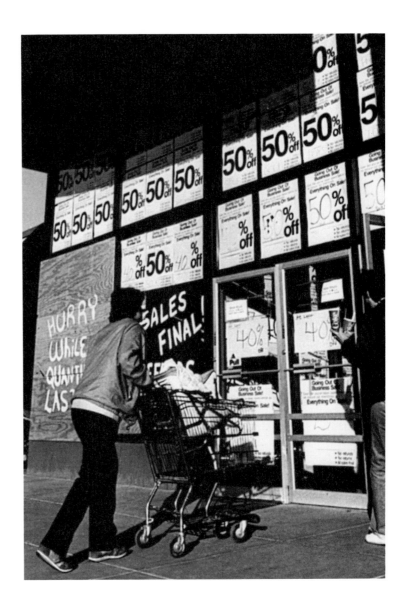

When stores have sales, they often want to reduce their inventory.

What Happens When Prices Are Below the Equilibrium Price?

As a consumer, you probably believe that prices are never low enough. But what do you think happens if sellers price a good or service below the equilibrium price? Buyers will want to buy more than is available.

When this happens, there is a shortage. A **shortage** means that buyers want to buy more than sellers are willing to offer for sale at that price.

Suppose that in Cal's effort to sell his surplus T-shirts, he lowers the price to $10. Now people are willing to buy more of his Custom T's. Suddenly he doesn't have enough T-shirts to keep up with demand. Therefore, he will probably raise his prices again. Eventually, he will find that at $20 each, he and the consumers agree. He is at the equilibrium price. There are no surpluses or shortages. Graph 5.4 shows a supply curve and a demand curve for Cal's Custom T's. At prices below $20, the equilibrium price, shortages exist.

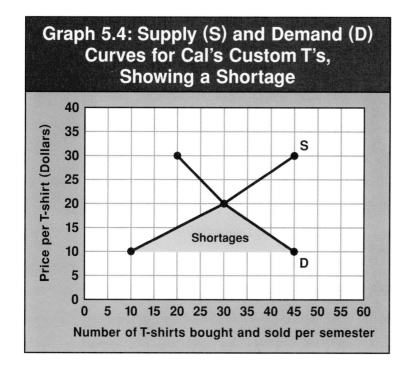

Graph 5.4: Supply (S) and Demand (D) Curves for Cal's Custom T's, Showing a Shortage

At any price below the equilibrium price, shortages exist.

Great Economic Thinkers: Alfred Marshall

**Alfred Marshall
(1842–1924)**

Alfred Marshall was a famous economist who was born near London, England, in 1842. He is well known for his ideas about supply, demand, and equilibrium prices. He wrote about supply and demand and how prices are determined. He was one of the first to describe these ideas as they are presented in this chapter.

When Marshall was in school, he loved math and was a very good student. This probably helped him to become a good economist later. He became an economics professor at Cambridge University in England.

In 1890, Alfred Marshall published a book called *Principles of Economics*. This was used as a textbook in economics classes for more than 50 years. It was also read by many people who were not students, but who just wanted to learn about economics. This book describes Marshall's ideas about supply, demand, and prices. It has influenced the way people think about supply and demand today as well as 100 years ago.

Alfred Marshall died in 1924. His *Principles of Economics* is thought to be one of the greatest economics books of all time. This gives Marshall an important place in the history of economics.

Chapter Review

Chapter Summary

- In a market economy, the forces of supply and demand set prices.

- The equilibrium price is the price at which consumers buy all they want and sellers sell all they want.

- When the amount producers supply is greater than the amount consumers want to buy, there is a surplus of goods and services. Producers often have to lower prices to get rid of the surplus.

- When the amount consumers want to buy is greater than the amount producers will supply, shortages result. Producers often raise prices to help meet production costs for the greater demand.

Chapter Quiz

Write answers to the following questions on a separate sheet of paper.

A. Thinking About Economics

1. What is the equilibrium price?

2. What causes surpluses?

3. When there is a surplus, what might producers do?

4. What causes shortages?

5. When there is a shortage, what might producers do?

6. Suppose the price of all brands of aspirin goes up. Do you think consumers will respond greatly to this price change? Give at least one reason why.

Graph 5.5: Supply (S) and Demand (D) Curves for Sally's Hamburgers

Price per hamburger (Dollars)

Number of hamburgers bought and sold per day

Use Graph 5.5 to answer the following questions.

7. At what price do the supply curve and the demand curve meet?

8. At this price, how many hamburgers will Sally produce?

9. At this price, how many hamburgers will Sally's customers buy?

10. Suppose Sally priced her hamburgers at $3 each. Would a surplus or a shortage exist? Why?

B. Personal Economics

When consumers think prices are too high, they will sometimes *boycott* a good or service. This means that they stop buying it. Why might this help lower the price?

C. World Economics

Japan is a country that doesn't produce a great amount of beef. It doesn't have vast areas of open range land and huge herds of cattle as does the United States. Also, the Japanese don't allow very much beef from the United States and other countries to be sold in Japan. So beef is not as big a part of the Japanese diet as is fish, for example. If there was a shortage of beef in Japan, how would you expect the price of beef to react? Explain.

Unit Two Review

Write answers to the following questions on a separate sheet of paper.

1. What law states that consumers are willing and able to buy more of a good or service when the price goes down?

2. What is the difference between complementary goods and substitute goods?

3. Give an example of complementary goods and substitute goods?

4. What law states that businesses are willing and able to produce more of a good or service as the price goes up?

5. Give two examples of production costs for a tomato grower.

6. Suppose the price of fertilizer goes up. How might this affect the amount of tomatoes supplied?

7. What is the equilibrium price?

8. Suppose there is a shortage of cotton at the current price. What might cotton growers do to the price of cotton? Why?

9. Suppose there is a surplus of cotton at the current price. What might cotton growers do to the price of cotton? Why?

10. Suppose the price of bubble gum goes up. How might consumers respond to the price change in terms of how much they buy? Why?

The American Economy at Work

American Business

Many Americans dream of owning their own businesses. Is it part of your dream?

Chapter Learning Objectives

- Explain the circular flow of income.
- Explain why profit is important in American business.
- Compare and contrast the three types of business ownership.

Words to Know

board of directors   a group of people elected by stockholders to make major decisions for a corporation

circular flow of income   the flow of payments for goods and services between households and businesses

corporation   a business that is owned by stockholders

dividend   a share in a corporation's profit that is paid to a stockholder

franchise   a business arrangement in which a large business chain, such as a fast food company, allows another person or group to operate an outlet using its name to sell goods or services

losses   what happens when a producer's total costs are greater than total revenues; the opposite of profits

partnership   a business that is owned by two or more people

revenue   money brought in by a business

sole proprietorship   a business owned by one person

stock   a share of ownership in a corporation

stockholder   a person who buys stock in a corporation; shareholder

Jan wakes up to a horn honking. She is late for work again. As quickly as she can, she gets ready and rushes to catch her ride.

Jan waits tables at the Courtyard Restaurant. This morning, her boss is angry. "Late again? I'll dock your pay this time, Jan," he scolds. "When you're late, the customers aren't happy. When the customers aren't happy, the business loses money. Around here, you only get paid for what you do."

Jan works extra hard that day. It's payday, and she's glad. That evening, she pays some bills. She writes checks for business school tuition and her share of the rent. She wishes she had some money left over for new clothes. But she'll have to wait for another paycheck.

That evening, she and her friend Patrick go out to a movie. "Let me buy us something to eat," he suggests afterwards.

When Patrick drives up in front of the Courtyard Restaurant, Jan begins to laugh. "You want to eat here?" she giggles. "Well, I can't say it's a bad idea. And while we're here, maybe I can wait on some tables. I could sure use some new clothes."

"Huh?" says Patrick. "What are you talking about?"

The Circular Flow of Income

The story of Jan and Patrick shows the **circular flow of income** in the economic system. Like Jan, you live in a household that buys goods and services from businesses. You buy food from stores and restaurants. You pay rent to a landlord for your apartment, or you make payments to the bank for your home. You go to ball games and movies for fun. You pay your income to businesses in exchange for goods and services.

Where did you get the income? Most people get their income from working for businesses. Through their jobs, they sell their labor. In return, they get wages. And where did the businesses get their income to pay the wages? From consumers like you and your family, when you buy goods and services. This process is called a circular flow of income.

Economics Practice

Write answers to the following questions on a separate sheet of paper.

1. Have you or your family contributed to the circular flow of income this week? Describe how.

2. Suppose you buy some shoes. How are you helping to put dinner on the table for the salesperson?

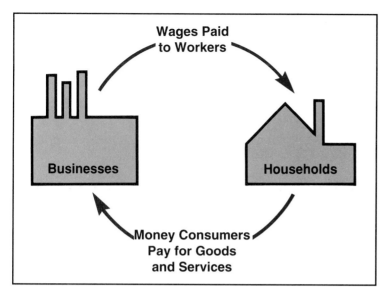

The Circular Flow of Income

The Profit Incentive

Businesses are the result of hard-working entrepreneurs. Entrepreneurs helped farm the New World, establish the fur trade, and map important transportation routes. Some of today's entrepreneurs may tinker with electronic notebooks. Others may build baby strollers for joggers or develop hair mousse for men. Remember that an entrepreneur is a person with ideas and a willingness to take risks. In return, most entrepreneurs or business owners hope to make a profit. In the United States market economy, profit is an important incentive for starting a business.

Making profits is not always easy. Any money that a business brings in is called **revenue**. Usually, this revenue comes from selling goods and services. For example, a bookstore brings in revenue from selling books or a shoe store from selling shoes.

Businesses use their revenues to pay for their costs in producing goods and services. This revenue must pay for natural resources, labor, and capital. The business owner hopes there will be enough left over to pay him or her a profit. Profits are the difference between total revenues and total costs.

In a free market economic system, people can start their own businesses whenever they want to. That is, as long as they don't break any laws. Of course, there is no guarantee that new businesses will make profits. Starting a business can be very risky. For years a business may show **losses** instead of profits. Sooner or later, the time comes when the business can no longer continue to operate. In fact, more than half of all new businesses fail in the first five years. But the dream of owning a business and earning profits provides incentives to people to keep trying.

Many people start small businesses because they want to "be their own boss."

Economics Practice

Write answers to the following questions on a separate sheet of paper.

1. Name two incentives for starting a business in America.

2. Give one drawback to owning a small business.

3. Explain why not all of the revenue coming into a business is profit.

The Three Types of Business

When a person takes the plunge and starts up a business, there are many things to decide: what to produce, how to produce it, and how to sell it. Just as important, the entrepreneur must decide how the business will be set up. There are three main choices:

- sole proprietorship
- partnership
- corporation

These types of business firms are owned in different ways. Each has its advantages and disadvantages.

Sole Proprietorships

At the beginning of the chapter, you read about Jan. Suppose she finishes school and decides it's time to start her own restaurant. She might choose to own it herself. A business owned by one person is called a **sole proprietorship**.

Out of approximately 17 million businesses in the United States, there are about 12 million sole proprietorships. Starting a sole proprietorship is often not complicated. Jan wouldn't need anyone's permission. She can start her own business or take over an existing one. Of course, she'll need to follow all laws, such as those regarding health and safety. Once she's in business, Jan will be her own boss. She'll be able to make her own decisions. She'll have control, which she never had as a waitress. And if she makes a profit, it will be hers alone.

But after several months, Jan may discover that there are some drawbacks to a sole proprietorship. There may be much more work than she can handle. And she may wish she had more money to help improve the business. Also, if someone were hurt in the restaurant, Jan could be sued. As the owner of the business, she would have to pay for the damages.

Partnerships

To solve her problem, Jan decides to bring her old friend Patrick in as part-owner. Whenever a business is owned by two or more people, it is called a **partnership.**

In the partnership, Jan and Patrick divide up the work. Each specializes in what he or she does best. Jan handles the bookkeeping and food planning. Patrick takes care of the hiring, scheduling, and training of employees. Jan likes the fact that Patrick has put some of his own money into the business. But she must share the decision-making—and the profits—with Patrick.

The large oil company that owns this tanker is a corporation.

Corporations

Jan and Patrick have a good small business going. They work well together, and they enjoy running their own business. They decide it's time to expand and start a small chain of restaurants. They also decide that it would be a good idea to make their business a corporation. However, starting a corporation is a complicated legal procedure. Many papers have to be filed with the government. So Jan and Patrick hire a lawyer to help them.

A **corporation** is a business that has been divided into shares of **stock.** These shares are owned by **stockholders** or shareholders. The buyers of the stock become shareholders. They are now part owners of the business. Owning stock can entitle the holder to a part of the year's profit—although it doesn't guarantee it. Often a corporation may decide to distribute some of its profit to stockholders in the form of a **dividend**.

Selling stock gives Jan and Patrick money to put into their restaurant chain. The business grows successfully. The stockholders have elected a **board of directors**. This group of people makes important decisions for the corporation. It appoints the managers and decides what to do with the profits.

The future of this corporation looks very bright. But as the business has grown, it has changed a lot. Jan and Patrick now find that they no longer enjoy the business. They miss the old days when they knew each of the customers personally. Finally, they may decide to sell their shares of the corporation and get out of the business altogether. But they will have some satisfaction knowing that the corporation can go on without them. They may then go on to start a new small business with the money they have made.

Besides the opportunity for growth, corporations have some definite advantages over other types of business firms. In sole proprietorships and partnerships, the owners can be sued. If they lose the lawsuit, they can lose all of their personal property as well as the business. But the law looks at a corporation as though it were a person. If the corporation is sued, the stockholders or owners would not lose any of their personal property.

Corporations make up only a small part of the businesses in the United States. Yet they bring in most of the business revenue.

A large corporation such as General Motors can bring in billions of dollars in revenue in a year, and still not show a profit. Can you explain why?

On the other hand, a problem with corporations is that profits are taxed twice. The business pays taxes on its profits. And the individual stockholders who receive dividends must pay taxes on their dividends. Another disadvantage is that stockholders in many corporations may have little say in how the company is run. Still, if a business wants to improve and grow, becoming a corporation may be an intelligent choice.

Type of Business Firm	Advantages	Disadvantages
Sole Proprietorship	• Owner has control. • Owner can use all profit as sees fit. • It's easy to start the business.	• Sometimes it's hard to raise money. • Owner is responsible for the success or failure of the business. • Owner takes personal risk of being sued.
Partnership	• Partners share work. • Partners can contribute money to help the business succeed.	• Partners sometimes disagree. • Profits must be shared. • Owners take personal risk of being sued.
Corporation	• Money is raised through sale of stock. • Stockholders have no risk of losing personal property if corporation is sued.	• Corporate profits can be taxed twice. • Corporations are hard to set up. • Stockholders may have little say in how the business is run.

Economics Practice

Use the table on page 78 to answer the following questions. Write your answers on a separate sheet of paper.

1. What type of business would suit people who want to do things their own way?

2. What type of business would suit a company that needs a lot of cash to grow?

3. What types of problems might partners have in a business? List at least three.

Learn More About It: The Franchise

Suppose you want to own a business, but you're just a little nervous about starting from scratch. You might want to consider buying and running a **franchise**. McDonald's fast-food restaurants are probably the best-known examples of franchises in the world today.

Here's how a franchise works. You (the *franchisee*) contract with a large, well-known corporation. You agree to pay a fee and a part of the revenue from your business in exchange for using the company name and products. The company might help you find a location or give you marketing tips. McDonald's will even send you to "Hamburger University" to get a fast-food education.

The franchise is an interesting type of business firm. The franchise owner has the final responsibility for whether or not the business succeeds. But the parent company may have many rules and regulations that must be followed. By the same token, it can help the franchisee out in many ways. Some people think that owning a franchise is the best deal going in the business world.

McDonald's restaurants are among the world's most successful franchises.

Chapter Review

Chapter Summary

- Income flows from businesses to workers in the form of wages and back to businesses when consumers pay for goods and services. This is called the circular flow of income.

- In the American economy, the profit incentive encourages many people to start their own businesses.

- There are three main types of business firms: sole proprietorships, partnerships, and corporations. Each has advantages and disadvantages.

- Sole proprietorships give the owner control and decision-making power. But this type of business requires much work from the owner and lots of personal risk.

- Partnerships usually mean that the owners divide up the work, allowing each to specialize. Each partner usually brings money into the business as well. In turn, they share the profits and risks.

- In corporations, money is raised by selling shares of stock. A stockholder is a part owner of the business and may share in the decision making and a part of the profits. Profits may be distributed to stockholders in the form of dividends. If the corporation is sued, the stockholders cannot lose any of their personal property as they would in a sole proprietorship or partnership.

Chapter Quiz

Write answers to the following questions on a separate sheet of paper.

A. Thinking About Economics

1. How does income get from businesses to consumers?

2. How does income get from consumers to businesses?

3. What are two incentives for starting a business?

4. What is the difference between revenue and profit?

5. Suppose you own a restaurant. Where does the revenue come from?

6. Give three ways you'll have to use the restaurant revenue before you make a profit.

7. What type of business firm allows a person total control?

8. What is a possible drawback in a partnership?

9. How do corporations raise money to help the business grow?

B. Personal Economics

Of the three types of business firms, which would you like to have ownership in? Give at least two reasons why this type of business appeals to you.

C. World Economics

A multinational corporation is one which does business in several different countries. IBM, Xerox, and Ford are examples of multinational corporations. Some multinational corporations are small, but most are large.

a. Would you expect a corporation's revenue to increase or decrease if it begins doing business in different countries? Explain your answer.

b. Suppose the ABC Corporation opens offices in Germany and France. The cost of doing so is $5 million. The revenue which these foreign offices bring in is $7 million. Is the ABC Corporation making a profit from its offices in Germany and France? Explain your answer.

Chapter 7

Stocks and Bonds

The New York Stock Exchange is the largest in the United States. Why do you think so many people invest their money in stocks?

Chapter Learning Objectives

- Explain two ways a person can make money on the stock market.
- List two different kinds of stock.
- Describe what a bond is.
- List two responsibilities of the Securities and Exchange Commission.
- Give four guidelines for people thinking about investing in stocks or bonds.

Words to Know

bond   an IOU. The person who buys a *bond* is lending money to the government or corporation that sells the bond. The bondholder earns interest and is repaid at a specified date.

capital gain   the money earned when you sell something for more than you paid for it

capital loss   the money lost when you sell something for less than you paid for it

common stock   stock that gives the stockholder voting rights but may or may not offer dividends

creditor   a person or business who is owed money

interest   a specified amount of money a borrower must pay a lender for the use of borrowed funds

invest   to use money to earn interest or income, or in the hopes of making a profit; for example, to buy stocks or bonds

investment   the use of money to earn interest or income, or to make a profit. In economics, *investment* often means spending by a business on capital goods.

preferred stock   stock that offers the stockholder stated dividends but does not give the stockholder voting rights

securities   stocks or bonds

stockbroker   a person who is licensed to buy and sell stocks and bonds for other people

stock market   a place where stocks and bonds are traded (bought and sold)

If I Had a Million Dollars . . .

A group of students were talking about what they would do with a million dollars.

"I'd buy a Ferrari and some new clothes," said Jillian.

"I'd buy my mother a house," said Fernando.

"I'd travel to Tahiti and never come back," said Lee.

Powell thought for a minute. "I'd put it in the stock market and make two or three million more," he said.

Stock is a share of ownership in a corporation.

"Then, since all of you had used up your millions, I'd take you out to lunch."

Powell thinks he has a great idea. He'll take his million, **invest** it in stocks, and get a high return on his money. But Powell has to remember that not everyone wins big on the stock market.

Stock Dividends

In Chapter 6, you read about Jan and Patrick's restaurant chain. They turned it into a corporation and sold stock to consumers. The people who bought the stock owned part of their restaurant company. In turn, they used the money to help their business grow. Profits made by the business were then distributed among the stockholders in the form of dividends.

Holding stock does not always mean you will get a dividend, however. If you buy **preferred stock**, you will receive a stated dividend each year. Many companies also pay dividends on their **common stock**. But if a company is short of money, people who own preferred stock get paid their dividends first. In this case, there may not be enough money for common stock dividends.

Common stockholders get to vote at yearly stockholders' meetings, while preferred stockholders do not. They can vote for such things as who will be on the board of directors.

If you want a safe dividend, does preferred or common stock seem like a better investment? Why?

Buying and Selling Stock

Another possible way to make money is through buying and selling stocks. Suppose that you invested $1,000. You bought 100 shares of Jan and Patrick's stock at $10 each. In three years, the chain does very well. It shows bigger and bigger profits each year. The stock is seen as a good **investment**. The laws of supply and demand drive the price up. It is now worth $30 per share. If you sold your 100 shares of stock, you'd get $3,000. This is $2,000 more than your initial $1,000 investment. The profit you make is called a **capital gain.** Now you wish you'd invested a million!

Anyone who invests in stock is taking a risk, however. Suppose the restaurant chain did poorly. The price of the stock would probably drop. If you had to sell your 100 shares of stock at $5 each, for example, you would only get $500. That's $500 less than you bought the stock for in the first place. The money you lost from your first investment is called a **capital loss.**

Due to the risk of losing money, many people prefer safer investments, such as a savings account. You won't make much money, but you don't have to worry about losing your investment. And your money will be earning a guaranteed rate of interest. **Interest** is the amount of money a borrower must pay a lender for the use of borrowed funds. In this case, the bank is the borrower and you are the lender.

Investors must pay taxes on capital gains. The capital gains tax is sometimes called the "tax of the rich." Why?

Some companies give shares of stock to their employees. How do you think this benefit helps build loyalty and good job performance?

Economics Practice

Write answers to the following questions on a separate sheet of paper.

1. What is one difference between common and preferred stock?

2. If you bought stock for $400 and sold it for $1,000, what would be the amount of the capital gain?

3. If you buy stock for $20 per share, then sell it for $2 per share, what is the amount of the capital loss?

Where to Buy and Sell Stocks

Stock is bought and sold through a **stockbroker.** You would buy shares of Chevron, for example, through a stockbroker rather than from a gas station. A stockbroker is licensed to handle sales between buyers and sellers. Usually, stocks are bought and sold in units of 100 shares or more.

Most stocks are traded in a **stock market.** The largest stock markets in America are the New York Stock Exchange (NYSE) and the American Stock Exchange (ASE). Both are located in New York City.

These stock markets seem to be filled with noise and confusion. Stockbrokers known as *floor traders* rush around shouting out buy or sell orders. Other brokers make and take phone calls. Nervous investors, hoping to make a profit, watch the constantly changing stock prices on an electronic screen.

Several times a day, TV and radio news reports tell how the market is doing. The "market" for most people means the *Dow Jones Industrial Average,* or "Dow," as it is often called. The Dow is based on the stock prices of 30 leading industrial companies. If the market is "up," it's a sign that people feel confident about business and the American economy. People have been buying stocks and bidding up the prices. If the market is "down," people have been selling their stocks for lower prices.

Stock market prices can hold steady over time, then change suddenly in a day. Prices in the stock market can respond instantly to news of major events such as wars and elections. Since these events often affect business, they often affect the stock market. Many times even false rumors are enough to send the market flying upward or tumbling downward.

A *bull* is someone who believes the stock market is headed higher. A person who believes the market is headed lower is called a *bear*.

Listen to the news today. Is the stock market up or down?

Investors can also buy what are called "over-the-counter" stocks through brokerage firms. These stocks are usually from smaller, less well-known corporations.

Stockbrokers need to keep current on business trends and constantly changing stock prices.

Economics Practice

Write answers to the following questions on a separate sheet of paper.

1. Do you think investing in stocks is risky? Why?

2. If you were interested in buying stocks, who would you contact?

3. Suppose you hear the market has been sliding downward for five weeks in a row. What might this trend indicate?

Investing in Bonds

Consumers can also invest their money in bonds. Like stocks, bonds are sold on exchanges and through brokers. **Bonds** are basically a way for a corporation or government to borrow money. The organization selling the bond agrees to pay the buyer interest on the borrowed money over time. The full amount is then paid back later at a specified date. This date is called the *maturity* date. For example, let's say you bought a new 10-year bond with a 10% rate of interest. The purchase price was $1,000. You would earn about $100 interest per year for 10 years. You would also be repaid your $1,000 at the end of 10 years.

The bond buyer or bondholder doesn't own a part of a company. The bond buyer becomes a **creditor**— a person who is owed money.

Many bonds are issued by the federal, state, and local governments. Voters often see bond *initiatives* on their local or state ballots. These initiatives are the government's way of asking for permission to borrow money by selling new bonds. The government might need the money to improve roads, build a ballpark, or finance new jail services. Often, elected officials say that bonds are a good way to get money without raising taxes. But remember that borrowed money will have to be paid back, sometimes through tax revenues.

Buying bonds is usually safer than investing in stocks. But it still involves more risk than putting money into a savings account. The prices of bonds tend to go up and down, although not nearly as much as stock prices. The bond buyer is guaranteed the face value or dollar amount of the bond when it reaches maturity. But suppose the bondholder needs to sell the bond for some reason before that date. The bondholder may have to sell the bond at a price lower than the original purchase price.

Bonds issued by companies that are having serious financial problems are especially risky. These bonds often pay a very high rate of interest. But if the company should go out of business, the bonds could become worthless. The bondholder wouldn't just stop receiving interest payments. He or she would also lose all the money that had been invested. On the other hand, many people believe U.S. government bonds are one of the safest investments you can make.

Which would you rather invest in, stocks or bonds? Why?

Money raised from selling bonds is often used by the government to improve public services, roads, and buildings.

The Securities and Exchange Commission

Suppose someone inside a certain company told you that its stock was going to skyrocket in value. You could buy thousands of shares of stock and make a lot of money. Or could you?

It would be up to the Securities and Exchange Commission (SEC) to decide. The SEC is a federal government agency. It regulates the trading of **securities** such as stocks and bonds. This means that

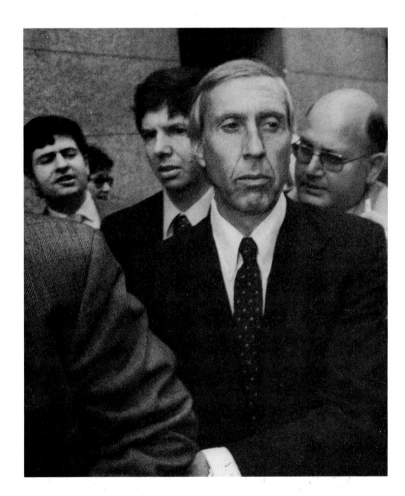

Ivan Boesky, who made millions trading stocks on inside information, on his way to jail

it enforces federal laws pertaining to stocks and bonds. The SEC tries to prevent people with "inside information" from making money unfairly on the stock market. It requires any organization issuing stocks and bonds to register with the federal government and outline its plans. If a business looks like just a crooked scheme to take investors' money, the SEC investigates.

Guidelines for Investing in Stocks and Bonds

If you had some extra cash, would you consider buying stocks or bonds? By now you know that the market involves risks. To minimize your risks:

1. Ask friends and other people you know about stockbrokers. Get the name of a broker you can trust.
2. Part of a broker's job is to give advice. But brokers are not fortune tellers. They cannot always predict which stocks will do well. Think over your broker's advice carefully.
3. Corporations will provide you with information about stocks or bonds being offered for sale. They will explain exactly how they plan to use the money raised. They will give figures on how well their businesses are doing. They will also give the rate of return on stocks in the past.
4. Be aware of what is happening in the stock and bond markets. There have been times when people's fortunes have been lost in an instant.

Learn More About It: Reading the Stock Report

Look at the stock reports in a newspaper. There are thousands of stocks and numbers in tiny print. With a magnifying glass and a little information, you can figure out these reports yourself.

This is a magnified section of the printed stock report found in newspapers. Here's how to interpret the headings:

Stock	52 Week High	Low	Div	Sales Hds	Last	Net chg
Imagico	28	18	1.00	47	27	$+1\frac{1}{4}$
Vivir	11	5	2.12	1239	7	-2

Stock reports are listed in newspapers.

Stock: The abbreviated names of stocks are listed alphabetically under this column. A stockbroker can tell you what company it refers to. If the letters *pf* appear after the stock name, it is preferred stock. Find Imagico stock. Is it preferred stock or common stock?

52 Week High/Low: This tells you the high and low price of each share of stock during the last 52 weeks. Imagico stock sold at a high of $28 per share. What was the low price?

Div: This stands for the annual dividend paid per share. The last dividend paid to stockholders of Imagico was $1 per share.

Sales Hds: This stands for sales in hundreds. In other words, add two zeros to the number listed to find how many shares were traded that day. In this case, 4,700 shares of Imagico were traded that day.

Last: This tells you the last price of the stock when the market closed that day. Imagico "closed" at $27 per share.

Net chg: This stands for net change. It tells you whether the stock increased (+) or decreased (−) in price and by how much from the previous day. Imagico increased by $1.25 from the day before. How did the price of Imagico change compared to Vivir? Explain your answer to a classmate.

Chapter Review

Chapter Summary

- People invest in stocks to make money. Income can be earned through stock dividends. Profits can also be made through buying and selling stocks as they go up and down in price. Trading stock for profit is sometimes a risky way to make money. There are no guarantees of high profits.

- There are two kinds of stock: *common* and *preferred.* Preferred stockholders receive stated dividends. Some companies also pay dividends on their comon stock. Sometimes a company may decide it needs to stop making dividend payments. In this case, common stock dividends are the first to be lowered. Common stockholders can vote in the yearly stockholders' meeting. Preferred stockholders have no voting rights.

- A *bond* is a lending agreement between a corporation or government and the bond buyer. The organization issuing bonds agrees to pay interest to the bond buyer. It then pays back the borrowed amount after a specified period of time.

- Stocks and bonds are usually bought and sold through brokers on the stock and bond exchanges.

- The stock and bond markets are regulated by federal laws and the Securities and Exchange Commission (SEC). The investor must be careful to make wise choices and should always be aware of the market risks.

Chapter Quiz

Write answers to the following questions on a separate sheet of paper.

A. Thinking About Economics

1. What is the difference between common stock and preferred stock?

2. How can an investor make money buying and selling stock?

3. Where are most stocks bought and sold?

4. If more people are buying rather than selling a stock, which way do you think the price will go?

5. What is a bond?

6. How is money from selling bonds used by governments? Give two examples.

7. What is a stockbroker's job?

8. What are two things the SEC does?

9. What are three things investors should consider when investing in stocks and bonds?

B. Personal Economics

If you had the cash, would you risk it on the stock market? Why or why not?

C. World Economics

Suppose a foreign car company announces a new product. The car is high quality and less expensive than similar American models. How might this affect the value of stock in American car companies? Why?

Chapter 8

Competition

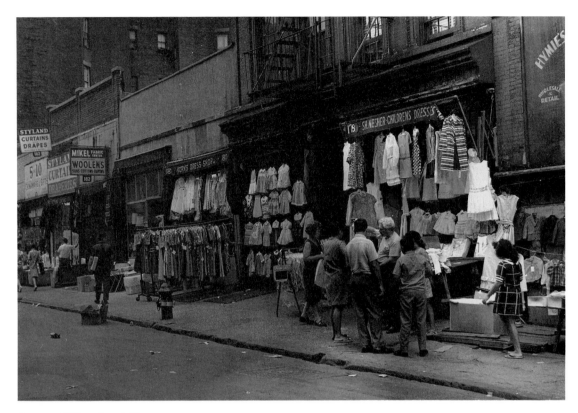

Competition is at the heart of the American economy. How do you think businesses such as these are able to compete with each other?

Chapter Learning Objectives
- List two reasons why competition is important.
- Identify two characteristics of perfect competition.
- Give three characteristics of monopolies.

Words to Know

competition   a situation in which producers or sellers of similar goods or services each try to get consumers to buy their products

monopoly   a business that has no competition; it produces a unique product or service

perfect competition   a situation in which there are a large number of buyers and sellers for the same product; supply and demand determine price

utility companies   businesses that provide vital services such as electricity, natural gas, and water; they are often government-regulated monopolies

warranties   written guarantees that products or services do what they are supposed to do

---

Jean and Harold are getting ready to drive to the beach for the day. "We're all set," says Jean. "I've got lotion, sandwiches, soft drinks, beach towels, and sunglasses. What else could we need?"

"Um, I need gas in the car," says Harold sheepishly. "Could you lend me five dollars?"

"This car is always empty," complains Jean. "I'll give you the money. But only if you buy the gas at my favorite gas station on 6th and Elm Street."

"What? That's ten blocks in the opposite direction! There's a gas station right on the corner. There are ten more stations on the way to the beach! Do you have your eye on some guy there?"

"No," says Jean with disgust. "It's just that I know that the people there are polite and give you good service."

Harold shakes his head. "Gas is gas. We're wasting our time."

"If gas is the same everywhere, how do all these gas stations stay in business?" argues Jean.

"Forget it," says Harold. "Hand over the money. We'll do things your way."

Economic Competition

Jean and Harold knew that gas was available at many gas stations. But they chose the one that they knew offered good service. All the gas stations are in competition with each other to get Jean and Harold to buy their gas. **Competition** is the rivalry between businesses that produce similar goods or services. Competition is a key force in the American economy. It does two important things:

1. It forces businesses to supply goods and services that people want. For example, suppose one company's running shoes aren't as good as those made by a competing company. The first business will probably have to improve its shoes or go broke.

2. It forces businesses to sell those goods and services at prices close to the cost of making them. For example, suppose two competing hamburger restaurants with similar quality burgers had very different prices. The one offering the better deal would get all the customers. The other hamburger restaurant would have to lower its price. This competition would go on until the price of both hamburgers was close to the cost of making them.

The degree of competition varies among industries. In some industries there is a great deal of competition. In others, there may be little or no competition.

Farm products, such as these pumpkins, come close to *perfect competition*.

Perfect Competition

Suppose that you decide to grow and sell pumpkins. You buy the seeds, plant them in your backyard, and watch them grow. Around Halloween, you harvest your crop and haul it to the farmer's market. You find dozens of other pumpkin sellers there and many people shopping for pumpkins.

The going price for pumpkins is ten cents per pound. You think about lowering the price to nine cents per pound, but why should you take less? You're confident you'll sell them all at ten cents per pound. You won't raise the price above ten cents either. The shoppers, seeing the difference, would go to your competition, the other pumpkin sellers. Supply and demand have set the equilibrium price at ten cents per pound. This is an example of perfect competition.

Perfect competition has these four characteristics:

1. There are many buyers and sellers. In the example above, there were numerous buyers and sellers of pumpkins at the farmer's market.
2. Producers are selling the same good or service. Pumpkins may vary a little in size and color, but they are basically identical.

Remember that the *equilibrium price* is the price at which the amount consumers want to buy is equal to the amount producers want to sell.

3. It is relatively easy for other producers to get into the same business. To get started, a pumpkin grower needs only land, seeds, water, gardening tools, and a little know-how.

4. It is easy to find information about prices, quality, and availability of the good or service. At the farmer's market, both buyers and sellers could easily see prices and quality. They could also see how many pumpkins were on sale that day.

Economics Practice

Write answers to the following questions on a separate sheet of paper.

1. What are two important ways in which competition helps consumers?

2. Economists often use the example of wheat as a product that offers perfect competition. Give one way that wheat matches a characteristic of perfect competition. Explain.

Monopoly

Suppose you owned the only hotel on a beautiful tropical island. The island is famous for its 37 waterfalls. That's why many people want to visit this special place. You control the supply of rooms and the rental price. There is no competition to think about. You have a monopoly.

A **monopoly** exists when there is a single seller or producer of a good or service. The seller controls supply and thus controls price. There is no competition to take away a monopoly's business by selling the good or service at lower prices.

Monopolies have three important characteristics:

1. There is only one producer. On the tropical island, you are the only one selling rooms for rent.

2. There is no substitute for the product or service. Visitors cannot stay in motels or campgrounds on the island because they don't exist.

3. It is difficult for others to begin selling the same good or service. Perhaps the costs are too high or resources are too limited. If you owned and governed your tropical island, you could simply not allow any other hotels to be built.

It may seem as if monopolies could charge any price they wanted to. For example, you may try to charge $1,000 a night for a room at your hotel. But what might happen? People could choose not to come. Sellers must pay attention to the demand for their product even when they have a monopoly.

Monopolies were pretty much outlawed in the United States when the Sherman Anti-Trust Act was passed in 1895. The government believed competition was needed to keep prices down and keep the economy healthy.

Monopolies do have their place in the United States, however. For example, most **utility companies** that supply electricity, gas, and water are monopolies. But they are regulated by the government. The government tries to keep the prices and level of services close to what they would be in competition. These monopolies are allowed because it would cost more and be impractical to have many utility companies in one area. Imagine trying to coordinate the wires and pipes of many different utility companies in one city!

What are the names of utility companies in your area?

Economics Practice

Write answers to the following questions on a separate sheet of paper.

1. Give two ways in which the battleship-building industry does not fit the characteristics of perfect competition. Explain.

2. If one company had a monopoly on computers, what might happen to the price of computers? Explain.

3. Why does it make sense to let the sewage disposal company in your town have a monopoly?

Other Types of Competition

Perfect competition doesn't exist in most industries. And monopolies are usually illegal or regulated. So how do most industries compete in the American economy?

In many industries, sellers of a good or service have some control over the price of their product. Remember that the pumpkin sellers did not. They had to sell their product at the going price of 10 cents per pound. Also, some products simply don't have large numbers of sellers and buyers. For example, you don't see rattlesnake venom on the grocery store shelves. Not that many people have a need for it. (And who wants to squeeze it out of the snake?)

No buyer or seller can know all about a product at all times. It would be next to impossible to check every store in town for the price of toothpaste. And few businesses are easy to start. A small pumpkin grower may not require much money or know-how. But try to start a car manufacturing plant and see what you run into! Starting up many businesses requires a great deal of money and information.

Rattlesnake venom can be sold to the medical industry to be used in making snake bite cures. How easy would it be to get into this business?

Cars, refrigerators, and washing machines are only produced by a small number of sellers. These industries are in between perfect competition and monopoly. Competition may be limited, in part because it's hard to start up a similar kind of business. These companies tend to keep each other's prices in check. If one company raises its prices, others may follow. If it lowers prices sharply, it may force the others to lower prices.

Have you ever heard of the word *oligopoly*? It exists when only a few sellers provide most of the goods and services in a particular industry.

How do airlines compete other than by offering lower prices?

A good example of this is the Big Three Auto Makers. The Big Three are General Motors (GM), Ford, and Chrysler. All together, they produce about 90% of the cars made by American companies. The products and prices are quite similar. So each company tries to get a competitive edge on the others. Each company tries to make customers think that its product is different, and better, than the others. A company may offer different auto-body styles or various types of **warranties**. But basically, the products are quite similar.

At the beginning of the chapter, there was a story about Jean and Harold. They were deciding what gas station to go to. Gas stations are an example of a business in which a large number of sellers offer similar products or services.

However, these products or services are not exactly the same, unlike the pumpkins in the perfect competition example. There may be dozens of gas stations in a city. They all sell gas. One may charge a little more or less than its competitors.

Businesses such as gas stations compete with one another by trying to make their product seem different. They also use advertising. You may see one gas station advertise itself as clean and friendly. Another gas station may advertise its all-night mechanic and high-octane gas. Still another may offer a lower price when customers pay with cash instead of using a credit card. Sometimes the location of a gas station is why people choose it over another.

Do you prefer one brand of toothpaste over another? What makes them different?

In the end, Harold is probably right. Gas is gas. But to many consumers, these slight differences in a product or service are very important.

DEGREES OF COMPETITION			
Number of Producers/ Sellers	Amount of Competition	How Easy or Difficult to Start Similar Business	Effect on Prices
Many producers	Perfect competition	Fairly easy	Prices do not vary between producers.
Many producers	Somewhat limited competition	Fairly easy	Prices between producers vary slightly.
A few large producers	Somewhat limited competition	Difficult	Prices are higher than if there were perfect competition; companies tend to keep each other's prices in check.
One producer	No competition; monopoly	Very difficult	Prices tend to be higher than when there is competition.

Economics Practice

Write answers to the following questions on a separate sheet of paper.

1. There are only a few large telephone companies that sell long-distance service. Is this perfect competition? Why or why not?

2. There are many small dry-cleaning businesses. Is this an example of a monopoly? Why or why not?

3. Most cereals are produced by a few large companies. How might one producer try to convince you to buy its oat-bran cereal instead of another kind?

**Adam Smith
(1723–1790)**

Great Economic Thinkers: Adam Smith

The year 1776 was filled with important events. The American colonies declared independence from Britain. James Watt built the first steam engine. And Adam Smith published one of the most famous economics books of all time. It was called *The Wealth of Nations.*

Adam Smith was born in Scotland in 1723. He was a good student and graduated from college when he was only 17. He was a professor for several years. Then he became a tutor to a very rich Scottish duke. This duke must have liked Smith a lot. He promised to give him a high yearly income for the rest of his life. Now Smith didn't have to worry about money. So he spent the next ten years writing *The Wealth of Nations.* He died in 1790 at the age of 67.

One of the things which Adam Smith wrote about was competition. He believed that competition was good for the economy. What happens when people or countries compete with each other? They end up producing the goods and services that other people want, at fair prices. This happens when people act in their own self interest. It's not because they're trying to be nice, or because the government tells them what to do.

For example, a baker doesn't produce bread just to make hungry people happy. The baker wants to make a living and earn a profit. He competes with other bakers to make his bread good enough and cheap enough so that people will want to buy it. Smith said that people like the baker act as if they are guided by an "invisible hand" to produce what people want to buy. In this way, Adam Smith said, when people follow their own self interest, it ends up being good enough for everyone else, too.

Chapter Review

Chapter Summary

- Competition forces businesses to sell goods and services that consumers want. It also forces businesses to keep prices at close to the cost of making the goods and services.

- When there is perfect competition, products are sold at the price determined by supply and demand. Perfect competition has the following characteristics:

  1. There are many buyers and sellers.

  2. Producers are selling products that are basically the same.

  3. It's easy for other producers to get into the same business.

  4. It's easy to find information about prices, quality, and availability of the good or service.

- A monopoly is a business that has no competition. Because of this, monopolies are able to charge higher prices for their goods and services.

- Most businesses are in between perfect competition and monopoly. Competition is limited, to varying degrees. In some industries, such as automobiles, a few large companies compete with each other. In other industries, many businesses compete.

- Sellers may compete in ways other than price, such as advertising.

Chapter Quiz

Write answers to the following questions on a separate sheet of paper.

A. Thinking About Economics

1. What is competition?

2. In which two ways is competition important?

3. When there is perfect competition, are there many or few buyers and sellers?

4. When there is perfect competition between businesses, is it fairly easy to start up the same kind of business? Why or why not?

5. Give an example of a product that fits the idea of perfect competition.

6. How might a monopoly affect prices?

7. Give an example of a legal monopoly. Why do you think it is allowed?

8. Give an example of an industry in which a few large companies provide similar goods or services.

9. Give an example of an industry in which a large number of small businesses provide similar goods or services.

10. How do businesses selling similar products try to win consumers? Give an example.

B. Personal Economics

Suppose that there are two grocery stores near your home. Both sell the same products. At one store, the clerks know you by name. They carry your groceries to your car. But prices at this store are slightly higher than at the other one. At which store do you think you'd do most of your shopping? Why?

C. World Economics

Many American companies compete with foreign companies. For example, Italian and Brazilian shoe companies sell their shoes in the United States. Suppose these foreign companies lowered the prices of their shoes. How do you think American producers might react?

Chapter 9

Workers and Wages

Workers are the suppliers of labor. Who provides demand for labor?

Chapter Learning Objectives

- Describe who makes up the labor force.
- Explain how the demand for goods and services affects the demand for labor.
- List three things that may affect wages.
- Explain how better capital resources can affect workers.

Words to Know

automation   the use of machinery, often computerized, in place of human labor

labor force   those 16 years old or older who are either employed or looking for work

minimum wage   the lowest hourly amount of money that a business can legally pay its workers

robots   electronic machines that are programmed to do tasks on an assembly line

wages   the price that businesses pay workers in exchange for labor

---

Lionel and Maria are looking for summer jobs. They apply at several fast-food restaurants, the city recreation department, and some grocery stores.

"I'm discouraged," says Lionel. "For every job we apply for, there seem to be a hundred other people applying, too. Most of these summer jobs don't pay a whole lot, either."

"I know," replies Maria. "It seems like all the high school kids in the city are looking for summer work now. I guess business owners can pay us low wages because there are so many of us willing to work."

Lionel wipes his forehead. "Well, I'll tell you something. I'm not going to put up with this for the rest of my life. Someday, people will beg me to work for them. They'll pay me well, too."

"Oh, really?" says Maria. "How are you going to do that?"

"I'm heading for medical school. I'll be a brain surgeon."

Maria nods. "I think you've got the right idea. Maybe we should be thinking about going to summer school if we don't get jobs at Burger Heaven!"

Supply, Demand, and Wages

The Department of Commerce estimates that there were about 125 million people in the U.S. labor force in 1990.

Lionel and Maria are discovering some important facts about how wages are determined. For the most part, wages—like prices—are determined by supply and demand. People in the **labor force** are the suppliers of labor. In the United States, the labor force is defined as people 16 years old or older who are employed or looking for work. Corporate executives, secretaries, chefs, and gardeners are all part of the labor force. So are people like Maria and Lionel—those who want jobs but haven't found them yet. People who choose not to look outside the home for work, such as homemakers or retired people, are not counted in the labor force.

On the demand side are businesses. They demand, or want to hire, a certain number of workers. A small store may only require a few clerks, while a large corporation may employ 10,000 workers. **Wages** are the price that businesses pay for labor. This price is usually determined by the supply of and the demand for workers.

In Unit Two, you learned that many things can affect supply and demand—and therefore prices. Likewise, wages can be affected by changes going on in the economy. Being aware of these changes can help you prepare for your role as a worker. Like Lionel and Maria, you can take certain steps toward getting yourself a job with good wages.

How the Demand for Goods and Services Can Affect the Demand for Labor

At one time, young people in cities like Detroit could pretty much count on getting good jobs. There were lots of high-paying jobs at Detroit's automobile manufacturing plants. While the jobs were often hard and boring, they usually paid fairly well. And workers also felt that their jobs were secure.

But in the 1970's and 1980's, the demand for American cars has decreased. People were buying more foreign-made cars instead of cars made in Detroit. As a result, the major U.S. auto makers decreased their production of cars. This means that the demand for auto workers decreased as well. There were not as many auto industry jobs in Detroit as there were before.

This example shows how the demand for goods and services affects the demand for labor. When the demand for a good or service is high, then the demand for labor in that industry is high. When the demand for a good or service is low, then the demand for labor in that industry is low. For that reason, it is a good idea to try to plan for a career in a growing industry. For example, the percentage of older people in the population is increasing. That means there will be a greater demand in the future for retirement home workers and medical workers who specialize in older people's needs. Another growing industry is the field of electronics. Each day seems to bring new advances in home and business electronics. Think about the lastest CD players, alarm systems, and digital displays on car dashboards. If consumers continue to demand such items, it is likely that the demand for electronics engineers and technicians will be higher as well.

Economics Practice

Write answers to the following questions on a separate sheet of paper.

1. Who is counted in the labor force? Who is not?

2. Give one example of an industry that may have a greater demand for workers in the future.

3. Explain why there might be an increased demand for labor in that industry.

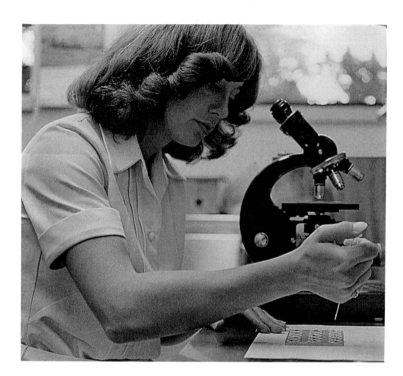

The demand for workers in the medical industry is expected to grow.

How Education and Skills Affect Wages

Workers in a certain industry do not always get high wages just because there is a demand for them. For example, there may be a great demand for fast-food workers. But wages in that field are not very high. This is partly because there are many people qualified to do those jobs. A large labor supply for an industry tends to mean lower wages for those workers.

Now think about the skills and education it takes to be a brain surgeon. Not many people have the time, money, qualifications and drive to pursue such a career. In part because of the limited labor supply, brain surgeons make very high salaries. Generally, the more education and skills a job requires, the higher the wages.

Years of School Completed	Median Income	
	Women	Men
High School:		
1–3 years	$13,538	$20,944
4 years	$18,042	$26,218
College:		
1–3 years	$21,328	$31,034
4 years	$27,654	$39,894

Median Income Compared to Years of Education Completed

(Source: Department of Commerce, Bureau of the Census, as reported in the *1994 Information Please Almanac*)

The table above shows the median income for year-round workers who were 25 years old or older in 1988. The word *median* means that half the population earns more than the listed income, and half earns less. The table compares that income to the number of years of education that the workers have completed.

Economics Practice

Use the table above. Write answers to the following questions on a separate sheet of paper.

1. Who tends to earn more: workers who haven't finished high school or those who have?

2. Who tends to earn more: workers who have some college, or those who have only finished high school?

3. Who tends to earn the most in any category: men or women?

How Productivity Affects Wages

Remember that productivity is the amount of goods or services produced in a given time period.

Another factor affecting wages is worker productivity. Workers who produce more per hour will often get higher wages than those who produce less. On one level, this may mean that the person who works the hardest gets the raise. On a broader level, it may mean that a company that is more productive will pay its workers higher wages.

Businesses often try to increase productivity by providing workers with better capital goods or resources. These can help increase a company's output of goods and services. For example, for many years secretaries used typewriters. Now word processing computers help secretaries produce more letters and reports at a faster rate. This increases the secretaries' productivity. If productivity is increased for the company, it may mean higher wages for the secretaries.

The secretaries have to learn new skills in order to increase their productivity and earn higher wages.

But sometimes these new capital resources can replace workers. For example, many automobile factories use electronic machines called **robots**. These robots now do many of the tasks once done by humans on the assembly line. Use of machinery or robots to replace human labor is called **automation.** Some automobile factories are now almost totally automated. The cars are almost completely put together by robots. Hundreds of people used to be needed in such factories. Now it takes fewer people working at computers that run the robots.

Do you think it's a good idea to use robots in factories? Why or why not?

There are many other examples of technology taking jobs away from people. Large farm machines such as the combine can do the work of many laborers. Fax machines may replace messengers who hand deliver papers. And some bank workers have been replaced by automated teller machines (ATMs).

It is important to remember that while such new technology eliminates some jobs, it also creates others. Think about the worker who once fastened bolts on an assembly line. This person might learn how to run and repair the machine that does that job now. Workers of the future must be willing to learn new skills as fast as technology changes. It is one way to ensure the best chances of having a job.

Economics Practice

Write answers to the following questions on a separate sheet of paper.

1. How can better capital resources help workers get higher wages?

2. Why do better capital resources sometimes force workers to learn new skills?

What It Means to Me: Minimum Wage

The government sometimes affects wages. For example, the United States government requires businesses to pay workers a **minimum wage**. Anything less than this hourly wage is illegal. The current minimum wage is $4.25 an hour. A person working 40 hours a week at the minimum wage would have a weekly income of $170.

In 1984, some members of Congress wanted to pass a *subminimum wage law*. It would have allowed businesses to pay teenagers $2.50 an hour from May 1 through September 30. This was less than the minimum wage at that time. Some lawmakers believed this would encourage businesses to hire teenagers for the summer. Many businesses said they weren't able to pay teenagers more than $2.50

In 1989 a new federal law created a below-minimum *training wage* for teenagers holding their first jobs. Very few businesses are using it. The current training wage is $3.62 an hour.

an hour for summer employment. If they had to pay more, they said, they wouldn't be able to hire as many teenagers. This would lead to higher teenage unemployment rates.

But some lawmakers argued against this idea. They felt it was unfair for businesses to pay adults and teenagers different wages based on age. Also, many adult workers with families might lose their jobs if businesses hired teenagers instead of adults.

The subminimum wage law was finally voted down. How would you have felt about such a law if it had passed?

Many teenagers work, especially in summer. Do you think they should be paid less than the minimum wage?

Chapter Review

Chapter Summary

- Wages, like prices, are often determined by supply and demand. People in the labor force are the supply; businesses who need workers are the demand.

- The demand for labor depends on the demand for goods and services. The greater the demand for goods and services in an industry, the greater the demand for labor. The less demand for goods and services, the less demand there is for labor.

- The more education and skills a job requires, the higher the wages. This is in part because fewer people acquire that level of education and skill. This creates a shortage of labor and drives up wages.

- Wages are also affected by productivity. Generally, higher productivity means higher wages.

- Better capital resources such as computers can often help workers to be more productive. Occasionally, workers are replaced by new technology. As a result, workers must keep their skills current with what is happening in an industry.

Chapter Quiz

Write answers to the following questions on a separate sheet of paper.

A. Thinking About Economics

1. What is the labor force?

2. Who is not included in the labor force?

3. How are wages determined?

4. Suppose that many working couples are having children. How do you think this might affect the demand for child-care workers?

5. Suppose that people buy less sugar. How might this affect the demand for sugarcane farmers?

6. Why do jobs that require a lot of education and skills usually pay high wages?

7. What is one way that businesses help their workers to be more productive?

8. How can better capital resources help workers?

9. Give one example of workers who have lost their jobs because of better capital resources.

10. What is one new type of job that has been created by technology in the last ten years?

B. Personal Economics

Suppose that someone asks your advice about whether or not to stay in school. What can you tell that person about the relationship between wages and education?

C. World Economics

In recent years, many companies in Japan have begun using robots in their factories. Some factories are almost completely run by robots. Japan is way ahead of the United States in the use of these machines. Why do you think the Japanese might be so eager to rely on robots in their factories?

Chapter 10

Labor Unions

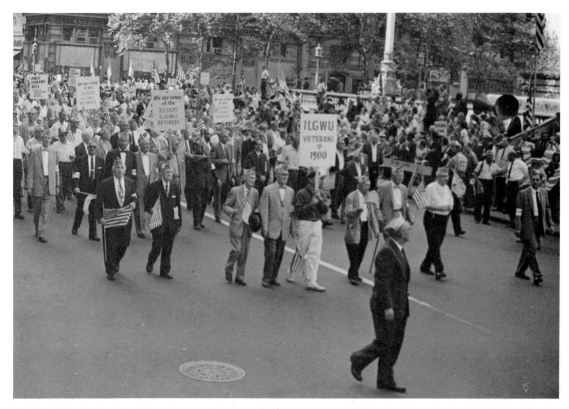

On the first Monday in September, we celebrate labor's contribution to the country. Labor Day parades take place all across America.

Chapter Learning Objectives

- Give two reasons why labor unions were formed in the United States.
- Explain three kinds of union memberships.
- Describe three ways that labor and management reach agreements.
- Describe current membership trends in labor unions today.

Words to Know

agency shop   a business in which employees are not required to join a union but must pay union dues

arbitration   a process by which an outside party decides the terms of an agreement that must be accepted by both sides in a labor dispute

boycott   a refusal to buy goods or services until an agreement is reached

closed shop   a business that only hires workers who already belong to a union

collective bargaining   a process by which management and labor reach agreements through negotiation and compromise

fringe benefits   any benefits given to workers other than wages, such as vacation pay, sick leave, pensions, and so forth

labor union   an organization that fights for workers' rights, wages, and benefits in a particular industry

lockout   the closing of a business by management to force workers to accept terms of an agreement

right-to-work laws   state laws which give people the right to work without belonging to a union

scab laborers   workers who cross a picket line to do the jobs of striking workers

strike   a work stoppage by labor to win terms of an agreement

union dues   dues paid by workers to support the union

union shop   a business at which employees must join the union after a certain period of time, usually 60 or 90 days

---

It's the first Monday in September. The parks are full of people picnicking, playing baseball, and sunning themselves. The Wallace family talks while they barbecue chicken on a grill.

"Labor Day is so sad," says 14-year-old Jim. "It means the end of summer and the beginning of school."

"I never understood why it's called Labor Day," comments his 12-year-old sister, Jill. "Nobody works. Everybody is relaxing."

"I guess I'd better explain it to you," said their father. "Labor Day is all about honoring the contributions that workers have made to this country. This holiday began in 1882 at the suggestion of Peter J. McGuire, a leader of the Knights of Labor. The Knights of Labor was the great-grandfather of many of today's labor unions."

"That's great, Dad," says Jim. "Is the chicken done yet?"

"You'll be better off learning about labor unions than eating chicken. Maybe it's time for a lesson."

"So why do we have labor unions, Dad?" asked Jim.

"What is a labor union?" asked Jill.

The Rise of Labor Unions

One hundred years ago, young people like Jim and Jill might have been part of the labor force. At that time, many workers endured unsafe conditions, long work days, and poor wages. There were no laws against child labor. Children often worked alongside adults in places such as coal mines.

Jim might have had to sort lumps of coal from dawn until dusk for only pennies a day. His father may have worked inside the coal mine with him. For as many as 12 to 14 hours a day, he'd be inhaling deadly coal dust. This would eventually destroy his lungs.

To make ends meet, Jim's sister may have sewed clothing in a "sweatshop." In summer, the sweatshop would get so hot that many of the women and girls would pass out. Those who did would simply be kicked out onto the street until they could work again.

Many people worked under such horrible conditions. Workers eventually joined together in labor unions, in part to improve working conditions. A **labor union** is an organization that fights for rights, wages, and benefits for workers in a particular industry. Labor unions have been an important force in the United States since the 19th century. Up until that time, many people worked on farms or in very small businesses. But with the growth of industry and factories in the United States, many people moved from the farms into the cities. Businesses grew larger. They employed hundreds of workers to produce large quantities of goods and services. There was a large supply of *unskilled labor*. This enabled many businesses to pay workers low wages while they worked in poor conditions.

Many workers believed that if they joined together they could convince the management to improve their pay and working conditions. It was the job of management to keep costs down while producing as much as possible. Labor, made up of all the workers, wanted secure jobs, good wages, and good working conditions.

The modern labor movement began with the organization of the National Labor Union (NLU) in 1866. It was the first large organization to fight for the eight-hour work day. The NLU didn't last much beyond 1872. But it was followed by hundreds of unions that continued to fight for workers' rights. The Knights of Labor, founded in 1869, was a force in labor until about 1900.

In 1860 the average work week for a factory laborer was 66 hours. Today it is about 40 hours.

Early labor unions, such as the Knights of Labor, helped to lobby for child-labor laws.

Economics Practice

Write answers to the following questions on a separate sheet of paper.

1. What is a labor union?

2. What is the difference between *management* and *labor*?

3. Suppose you were working at a job 100 years ago. What kind of working conditions might you experience?

The Pros and Cons of Unions

In part because of labor unions' efforts, many workers in the United States now enjoy some or all of these benefits:

- an eight-hour work day and a 40-hour work week
- overtime pay (time and one-half) when working over eight hours per day

- health benefits
- medical care and compensation when hurt on the job
- vacation pay and paid sick leave

Not everyone believes that unions are necessary. Many people believe that individual workers could bargain on their own with management. Critics say that unions drive up production costs because they demand higher pay. This may result in higher-priced goods and services for all consumers. Others say that unions divide and disrupt companies. They believe that workers would earn the benefits they deserve by simply being as productive as possible.

Whatever your beliefs about unions, they are still an important part of the United States economic system. About 16 percent of all workers in the labor force belong to unions. The time may come when you will be affected by what a union does. For that reason, it's important to know how they work.

Do You Have to Join a Union?

Suppose that you go to apply for a job. You may be told that if you get the job, you must join a union. The local union represents the people in your particular plant, company, or geographic area. It is usually part of a larger national or international union which works on behalf of the local's needs.

Being a member of the union means that you will have to pay union dues. These **union dues** go toward supporting the union. The union believes that since it is working for the good of all employees, then everyone should pay dues. But you are not sure you want to join the union. Do you have to?

It depends. The type of union described in the example is called a **union shop**. It requires new employees to join the union after a certain period of

Do you think you might ever join a labor union? Why or why not?

time, usually 60 or 90 days. In an **agency shop**, employees do not have to join the union. But they do have to pay union dues.

If union shops and agency shops are legal in your state, then you probably must join in order to get this job. But if your state has right-to-work laws, then you do not. **Right-to-work laws** mean that people have the right to work *without* belonging to unions or paying union dues. A state's right to pass such laws came about in 1947 when the Taft–Hartley Act was passed. This act also outlawed closed shops. In a **closed shop**, only workers who were already members of the union could be hired.

Union members and non-union members can work in an *open shop*.

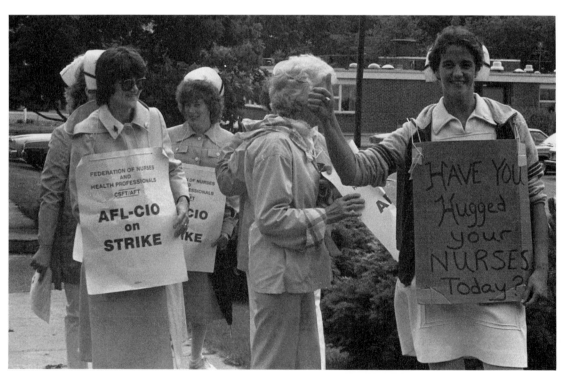

Calling a strike is often a last resort for unions. If you were a union member, do you think you would go out on strike if your union called for it? Why or why not?

Economics Practice

Write the answers to the following questions on a separate sheet of paper.

1. What are union dues?

2. What is the difference between a union shop and an agency shop?

3. What is a right-to-work law?

How Unions and Management Reach Agreements

As you know, the goal of many unions is to get fair wages and good fringe benefits for employees. These **fringe benefits** may include health care, vacation, sick days, and so forth. Meanwhile, management wants to keep costs down and production up while being fair to workers. How do these two sides ever agree?

Labor unions and management sit down and negotiate. Through **collective bargaining**, they state their goals and work out acceptable agreements. Often both sides must compromise.

Here is a simple example of what may happen in collective bargaining. Suppose the union asks for a 10-percent wage increase. Management says it can't afford it. They offer a 3-percent wage increase. The union says it will accept a 5-percent wage increase with an extra paid sick day for each employee per year. Management agrees. Each side has given up a little to reach an agreement.

Collective bargaining does not always go so smoothly. Sometimes, no agreement can be reached. In such cases, the union may call a **strike**. A strike is a call for all laborers to stop working until the union's demands are met. The workers walk a *picket line* to voice their opinions and keep scab laborers out. **Scab laborers** are non-union workers hired during a strike. Auto workers, steel workers, transportation workers, and others have used or threatened to use strikes to try to get what they want.

A union may also call for consumers to boycott a company. During a **boycott**, workers urge all consumers to stop buying the goods and services that the company produces. This tactic was successfully used by the United Farm Workers (UFW) in the 1970s. By encouraging consumers to boycott grapes, farm workers won better wages and working conditions from grape growers. Both strikes and boycotts are meant to put economic pressure on companies and force them to give in.

In some cases, management may try to force labor to agree to certain terms through a lockout. During a **lockout,** the company closes its doors to its workers. During the period while the business is closed, workers receive no wages. This might cause many workers to give in.

Strikes do not always work. For example, the strike by air-traffic controllers during the early 1980s resulted in many union members losing their jobs. During the long history of labor unions, there have also been many instances where strikes and lockouts have ended in violence. Today, labor and management try to avoid violence by using **arbitration**. This means that an outside party looks at each side's demands to determine a fair outcome. Usually, both sides agree to accept the arbitrator's decision, no matter what.

Economics Practice

Write answers to the following questions on a separate sheet of paper.

1. What are two methods that labor unions use to get management to meet their demands?

2. What is one method that management might use to get unions to give in?

3. What is arbitration?

What's Happening with Unions Now?

Unions have been losing membership and strength in the United States for the last 20 years. In 1970, 27.3 percent of the labor force belonged to unions. This figure had dropped to 15.8 percent in 1992. What is causing this trend?

Part of the decrease is the result of fewer jobs in certain industries. For example, the steel industry employs fewer workers than it did 20 years ago. So there are fewer people to join the United Steelworkers Union. This same trend can be seen in many manufacturing industries in the United States.

It may also be that people are deciding not to join unions like they used to. Perhaps they believe that unions no longer have the bargaining power they once did. Indeed, foreign competition from countries such as Japan and Korea has caused many unions to rethink their goals. These countries now sell many different types of goods in the United States. Often, these goods are equal or better in quality and lower in price than similar American goods. To compete, may American companies have had to keep their costs down and try to get worker productivity up. During the 1980s, many unions agreed to give up wage increases in exchange for job security.

This does not mean that unions are disappearing or giving up. Many unions are trying to maintain existing worker benefits, such as health care, instead of trying to increase them. Other unions are offering retraining for displaced workers. As the needs of the work force and the economy change, the unions must change, too.

Five Large Unions in America Today	
Union	**Membership**
1. Teamsters	1,700,000
2. American Federation of State, County, and Municipal Employees (AFSCME)	1,300,000
3. United Food and Commercial Workers	1,300,000
4. United Auto Workers (UAW)	861,658
5. Service Employees	1,000,000

(Source: *1994 Information Please Almanac.* Many unions in America, such as the UAW, belong to the AFL–CIO.)

Economics Practice

Write answers to the following questions on a separate sheet of paper.

1. What is the current trend in union membership?

2. Give one way in which unions are changing to meet changing economic conditions.

Learn More About It: The AFL–CIO

One of the strongest voices in American labor this century has been the AFL–CIO (American Federation of Labor–Congress of Industrial Organizations). The AFL–CIO is known as a *federation*. It includes more than 100 unions with about 14 million members.

At one time, the AFL and CIO were separate federations. The AFL was organized in 1886 under the leadership of Samuel Gompers. At that time, it mainly represented skilled craft workers. The CIO was founded in 1938 by John L. Lewis. In contrast to the AFL, it included mostly unskilled assembly-line workers as its members.

After the passage of the Taft–Hartley Act, which was seen as anti-labor, these two federations were drawn together. They formally joined in 1955. Since that time, the AFL–CIO has helped to pass many laws that favored the cause of labor. Politicians often seek endorsement by the AFL–CIO as a way of gaining workers' votes.

Chapter Review

Chapter Summary

- The first labor unions in America were formed in the last half of the 19th century. At that time, the country was rapidly becoming industrialized. Many growing businesses took advantage of the large supply of unskilled labor. Poor working conditions and low wages caused workers to unite for better work environment and pay.

- In some industries, employees may have to join a union, or at least pay union dues. This is not true in states that have right-to-work laws. These laws uphold a person's right to work without joining a union.

- Union dues are used to support the officials and activities of the local union and the larger national or international union. Unions use collective bargaining to negotiate wages and fringe benefits with management. If collective bargaining fails, unions may use strikes or boycotts to force an agreement. Management may try to force an agreement by using tactics such as hiring non-union laborers. Sometimes, the process of arbitration is used to find a peaceful solution.

- Union membership has declined in the last 20 years. This is partly due to the decrease in manufacturing jobs. Also, many workers no longer see unions as strong or needed. Still, unions are an important force in the economic system today.

Chapter Quiz

Write the answers to the following questions on a separate sheet of paper.

A. Thinking About Economics

1. What started the shift of labor from the farms to the cities?

2. What were working conditions like for many factory workers in the 1800s and early 1900s?

3. What are two things that unions have struggled to win for American workers?

4. Some people argue that unions drive up the cost of goods and services. Explain how this could happen.

5. How is an agency shop different from a union shop?

6. What was the Taft–Hartley Act?

7. What happens in collective bargaining?

8. What is the difference between a strike and a lockout?

9. Give one example of a successful boycott.

10. Give one possible reason why union membership has decreased in recent years.

B. Personal Economics

Suppose that you were asked to join a union. List two things you might want to learn before making your decision.

C. World Economics

In the last few years, a growing number of U.S. corporations have been moving their production to other countries. They have set up factories in such places as Mexico, Thailand, and Indonesia. Workers in these countries are willing to work for much lower wages than American workers. And American companies are legally permitted to hire them. What effect do you think this has on American labor? How are labor unions likely to react? Will the unions be put into a stronger or weaker bargaining position when negotiating with management? Explain your answer.

Unit Three Review

Write answers to the following questions on a separate sheet of paper.

1. In the circular flow of income, wages are paid by businesses to laborers. How does money get back to the businesses?

2. What is revenue?

3. What are the three main types of business ownership?

4. What is one reason that people invest in stocks?

5. To whom would you go if you wanted to buy stocks or bonds?

6. What is meant by perfect competition?

7. Why are utilities sometimes allowed to be monopolies?

8. When two businesses produce very similar products, how does each one try to get consumers to buy its products? Give an example.

9. Why would a business want to provide its workers with better capital goods or resources?

10. Why did many workers in the United States in the 19th century join labor unions?

The Role of the Consumer

Consumer Spending

Consumers usually shop around for the best prices when they buy major appliances for the home.

Chapter Learning Objectives

- Describe three steps in making spending decisions.
- List three ways consumers can learn about goods and services.
- Describe at least three things to consider when comparing quality, features, and price.
- Identify agencies that help protect consumer rights.

Words to Know

bait and switch an illegal form of advertising

Better Business Bureau a private organization that helps protect consumers from unfair business practices

budget a breakdown of how income is used; a personal plan for spending income

chamber of commerce a group of representatives of local businesses who meet regularly to promote business in their town or city

comparison shopping looking at similarities and differences in features, prices, and quality of competing goods or services

fraud deceit, trickery

full warranty a warranty that promises to replace or repair all parts at no cost for a certain period of time

generic without a brand name

limited warranty a warranty that promises to pay all or partial replacement costs on certain parts for a specified period of time

priorities things that come first in order of importance

Megan needs to buy a car. She's just been hired at a business that is on the outskirts of her city. Neither the bus nor the subway goes there. She has decided that it would be a good idea to buy a used car. She's been talking to sales people and friends, and she's also been doing some reading. Megan has narrowed her choices to two cars. Both have low mileage, are in pretty good condition, and have a price she can afford. One car is a little sportier and more expensive than the other. The less expensive car has lots more trunk room than the other model. Megan is doing some final thinking about what is most important to her in a car. She is almost ready to make her decision.

The Consumer's Choices

In earlier chapters, you learned that consumers such as Megan have an important role in the economy. They help determine what goods and services are on the market. And they help set prices through supply and demand.

However, many consumers do not feel important or powerful. In the United States, consumers have hundreds of thousands of goods and services available to them. There are mints, baseball gloves, aerobics lessons, insurance policies, french fries, and tofu burgers. And there are books, records, tapes, CDs, trucks, cars, umbrellas, amusement parks, and on and on. Most consumers cannot begin to pay for all of these things. They have a limited income that forces them to make choices. Often, consumers feel frustrated and confused about how to make spending decisions.

List the dozen or so goods or services that are the most important to you.

Like Megan, you can make spending decisions that will fit your needs, wants, values, and lifestyle. Just follow these three steps to make sound economic decisions that are right for you:

1. Set goals.
2. Gather information.
3. Think about the trade-offs, or opportunity costs.

This chapter will tell you more about these steps and how to follow them.

Step One: Set Goals

How can you set goals? First, make a list of your **priorities** and rank them from first to last. Is it more important to get your own apartment, or buy a car? Do you want to go to work right after high school, or travel for a while? Would you rather buy new clothes, or get your mother a birthday gift? Your priorities will depend on things such as your immediate needs, wants, and values. For example, Megan had to have a car for work. The car became a priority for her. But if she could have used public transportation, she probably would have done that. Owning a car in and of itself was not important to her.

When setting goals, it is also helpful to make a budget. A **budget** is a breakdown of how you spend your money. Subtract what you spend on necessities such as food, housing, utilities, and so forth from your income. The amount you have left over is what you have in your budget to spend on other goods and services. Budgets are a helpful way to think about your spending and figure out what you can really afford.

Suppose Megan made her budget. After subtracting what she spends on necessities, she found she had about $300 per month left. She set the realistic goal of buying a used car with payments of around $150 per month. This would leave her money for gas, insurance, a little entertainment, and savings, too.

Make a simple budget to see how you spend your money.

Monthly Income (after taxes)		$1,200.00
Expenses:		
Rent	600.00	
Utilities	50.00	
Food	150.00	
Clothes	100.00	
	900.00	900.00
Remaining Income		$ 300.00

This simple budget helped Megan see how much money she had for car payments.

Economics Practice

Write answers to the following questions on a separate sheet of paper.

1. How do consumers help themselves by listing their spending priorities?

2. Suppose a person makes $500 per month. Each month, he pays $200 in rent, $50 in utilities, and $150 for food. How much money does he have left for other spending?

3. Name a high-priority good or service that you want to buy.

Would you spend $2 in gas or 4 hours of your time to save $1 on the price of an item? Why or why not?

Step Two: Gather Information

Once you determine your priorities and budget, you can decide what you want to spend your money on. Begin by gathering information about competing goods and services. This is the start of comparison shopping. **Comparison shopping** means looking at the similarities and differences in quality, features, and price of things you are thinking of buying. To gather this information, you can read product labels, consumer magazines, and advertisements. You can talk to salespeople or your family and friends who've shopped for something similar. Here are some important things you must consider:

- *Does the product have a written warranty?*

  A *warranty* is a promise by the producer that the good or service will do what it is supposed to do. A written warranty that comes with a good or service should always be read carefully. A **full warranty** usually promises to repair or replace any part of a product for a certain period of time. A **limited warranty** may promise to repair or replace only certain parts of a good. And sometimes you, the consumer, will have to pay the labor costs involved in the repair. For example, suppose Megan's car had a limited warranty. The used-car dealer may have promised to replace only certain engine parts within 30 days or 3,000 miles.

- *Does the product have a brand name, or is it generic?*

Sometimes, consumers think they will get high quality just by buying a product from a well-known company. But sometimes **generic** products are just as good and they are usually less expensive. Generic products carry no brand name. They are usually plainly packaged. For example, you can find aspirin under many different brand names. And you can find generic aspirin which is simply labeled "Aspirin." By comparing ingredients, amounts, and prices on these products, you can determine whether the generic product is a better buy.

- *Where are you shopping?*

Different types of stores may offer the same product at different prices. In many large cities, consumers have the choice of shopping at small boutiques, large department stores, or factory outlets. Each type of store has its own advantages and disadvantages. A small, exclusive store will usually charge higher prices than a discount outlet. But you may get the added feature of personal customer service at the smaller store.

Sometimes you can get the best price by buying from someone you know well. For example, Megan may have chosen to buy a car from a friend. Usually, no warranty is in effect when you buy this way, however.

- *What additional costs will there be?*

Suppose that, like Megan, you buy a car. Suddenly you find that your spending has just begun. There are taxes and registration fees to pay. You must get insurance. And then there are those tune-ups and oil changes.

Before you buy something, consider what the additional costs will be. If these costs do not fit your budget, you may have to revise your goals.

Economics Practice

Write answers to the following questions on a separate sheet of paper.

1. What are three ways to learn about quality, features, and price?

2. Give an example of a limited warranty.

3. Suppose you are looking at clothing. The label on sweater "A" says it must be dry cleaned. Sweater "B" can go into the washer and dryer. Which will be less expensive in terms of additional costs? Why?

Step Three: Think About the Trade-offs

Now that you have all your information, make your comparisons. What will you be trading off or giving up when you buy one thing instead of another? In other words, what is the opportunity cost of your decision?

To help you with this process, it is a good idea to make a list of the things you are looking for. Then compare how competing goods or services measure up. By knowing exactly what you are getting and giving up, you can make an informed decision.

Here is what Megan's list might look like.

What I Want	Car A	Car B
Reliability	reliable	very reliable
Low mileage	45,000	37,000
Sporty looking	yes	no
Trunk room	no	yes
Under $5,000	$4,500	$4,200
Warranty	limited	limited

Economics Practice

Use Megan's trade-off list to answer these questions. Write your answers on a separate sheet of paper.

1. Which car is most reliable?

2. Which car has the lowest mileage?

3. Which car has the lowest price?

4. Suppose it is very important for Megan to drive a sporty looking car, and so she buys car "A." What will she be giving up or trading off?

Consumer Protection

Suppose Megan makes her decision. She goes for sporty car "A." Two weeks after she drives the car home, the transmission goes bad. The car dealer says he doesn't have to pay for the repairs. What can Megan do?

As a consumer in the United States, Megan has certain rights. These rights were outlined in a speech by President John F. Kennedy in 1962. They are:

- The right to choose among various products or services.
- The right to safety in consumer products.
- The right to be fully informed about the type of good or service.
- The right to be heard—consumers have a say about laws affecting them.

There are a number of private and government agencies that consumers can use to see that their rights are protected. Among private agencies are the **Better Business Bureau** and the local **chamber of commerce**. Both could put pressure on the car dealer to honor the warranty. And they can warn other consumers not to buy from that dealer. Megan might also try looking in the phone book under Consumer Protection Organizations. Quite often, private consumer groups offer advice and assistance to bewildered consumers.

There are many local, state, and federal government agencies that can help consumers, too. These agencies give consumers information, investigate consumer **fraud,** and prosecute offenders. To find such an agency, try looking in the white pages of your phone book under County or State Government Listings. Then look under the heading Consumer Complaints.

The table on the next page lists some of the federal government agencies useful to consumers.

If You Want	Call This Government Agency
to hear recorded information on safety of a variety of products, or want to report unsafe products	Consumer Product Safety Commission 1-800-638-2772
to complain about vehicle safety or get information on driving and safety issues	Auto Safety Hotline 1-800-424-9393
information on proper care and preparation of meat, poultry, and eggs	The Meat and Poultry Hotline 1-800-535-4555
information on consumer banking laws	Federal Deposit Insurance Corporation 1-800-424-5488

If You Want	Write This Agency
The Consumer's Handbook, a free catalog of government publications on health, budgeting, nutrition, and other consumer issues	Consumer Information Center Pueblo, Colorado 81009
to report mail fraud	Consumer Advocate U.S. Postal Service Washington, D.C. 20260
information on how to complain effectively	U.S. Office of Consumer Affairs Humphrey Building 200 Independence Ave. Washington, D.C. 20201

Economics Practice

Use the table to answer the following questions. Write your answers on a separate sheet of paper.

1. Suppose you suspect your car has a safety defect. The dealer won't listen to you. Which government agency might you call?

2. You have some chicken that you think might have been left in the refrigerator too long. You're wondering if it's safe to eat. Which agency might be able to help you?

3. Suppose you want general information about how to get complaints answered. To whom would you write?

What It Means to Me: Bait and Switch

Ads can be very useful for comparing features, quality, and price. But ads are not there just to inform consumers. They are there to get consumers to buy. Often ads promise us love, good looks, health, and happiness if we buy a certain product. Most consumers are smart enough to know that using a certain toothpaste will not drastically change their lives. But other kinds of ads use low prices to attract and trick consumers. These are called **bait and switch** ads.

Here's how it works. Suppose a mountain bike is advertised at a low price. This is the "bait" to get you into the store. Once in the store, you're told that the product is no longer available. The salesperson tells you that it was a cheap, poorly made bike anyway. He says that you'd be better off buying a higher-priced bike. He just happens to have an expensive bike on hand. This is the "switch."

Bait and switch is illegal. If you experience this, contact your state agency for consumer complaints.

Chapter Review

Chapter Summary

- Consumers must use their limited income to meet their needs and wants. To ensure spending decisions that fit individual needs, it helps to set goals, gather information about quality, features, and price, and think about the trade-offs.

- To set realistic spending goals, list priorities and write out a budget.

- Consumers can learn about quality, features, and price through a variety of resources. For example, they can read consumer magazines, read labels, and talk to family, friends, and salespeople.

- When comparison shopping, it is helpful to compare warranties, as well as brand-name and generic products. It is also a good idea to compare prices for the same product at different types of stores, and additional costs.

- By thinking about trade-offs or opportunity costs, consumers may get a clearer picture of what they are getting. They will also be more aware of what they are giving up when they choose one product over another.

- Consumers have rights. There are many private and government protection agencies that can give consumers information and help protect their rights.

Chapter Quiz

Write answers to the following questions on a separate sheet of paper.

A. Thinking About Economics

1. How does limited income affect consumer buying decisions?

2. How can a budget help you set spending goals?

3. How can listing priorities help consumers set spending goals?

4. What are three ways consumers can gather information about goods and services?

5. What is the difference between generic and brand-name products?

6. Give an example of an additional cost that consumers should consider when buying clothing.

7. Where you make a purchase can affect price. Give an example.

8. Why should you read limited warranties carefully?

9. What is one private organization that can help consumers?

10. How could you find a government agency that helps consumers?

B. Personal Economics

Suppose that, like Megan, you have found two cars that meet most of your requirements. One is sporty, and the other has lots of trunk room. Which would *you* choose? How does your choice fit in with your values and lifestyle?

C. World Economics

When Americans travel to foreign countries, they usually like to buy things to bring back with them. Suppose you are on a vacation in Mexico. You've heard that you can get good buys on leather goods there. So you decide to buy a leather jacket. Remember the three steps in making spending decisions. Which steps would you follow in Mexico? Do you think it might be difficult to follow any of the steps? Why or why not?

Chapter 12

Saving and Borrowing

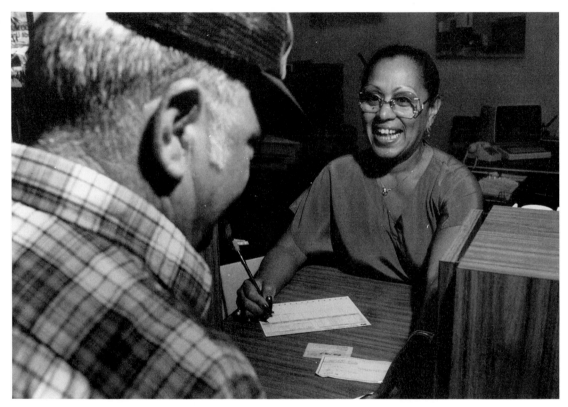

Why do you think it's better to keep your savings in a bank than at home under a mattress?

Chapter Learning Objectives

- Give two reasons for saving.
- Give two reasons for borrowing.
- Compare and contrast three different types of savings accounts.
- Explain what to look for when you shop for credit or loans.

Words to Know

annually   yearly

certificate of deposit (CD)   a type of time-deposit savings account for a fixed amount of money with a higher fixed interest rate than most other savings accounts

collateral   property or cash offered by a borrower as a guarantee that a loan will be repaid

compound interest   interest earned on the deposit and on all previously earned interest

credit   the promise to pay later for the purchase of goods or services without the actual transfer of money

financial institutions   banks, credit unions, savings and loans, and other organizations that offer services related to saving and borrowing money

money-market account   a savings account that requires a large minimum deposit

principal   in a loan, the original amount of money borrowed

time-deposit account   a savings account that requires money to be left in the account for a certain period of time

withdraw   to take out

Remember Megan from Chapter 11? Her car is now paid for. She's been working at the same job for three years. Megan's boss has suggested that she take a few evening classes so she can be promoted to manager. Little by little, Megan has been putting away money for tuition. Now she is considering taking out a student loan. She's hoping that in the long run, going back to school will help her make more money.

Like many consumers, Megan finds that saving and borrowing are helpful ways to meet her goals. By doing comparison shopping, you can find the best deals for earning interest on the money you save. And you can find ways to pay less interest when you have to borrow money. This chapter looks at some of the things that consumers should know about saving and borrowing.

Why Save?

People save their money for all kinds of reasons. Sometimes they save toward a big purchase, such as a down payment on a home. Sometimes they put away money for emergencies. Other times they save for their retirement or their children's college education.

Saving money can give you a sense of security. And it can help you meet your spending goals. How much you save depends on your income, budget, and goals. You may want to save 10 percent of your income on a regular basis. For example, let's say you get paid $100 per week. If you saved 10 percent of that, you'd be saving $10 per week.

Saving is also good for the economy. When consumers save, that money becomes available for businesses to borrow. This helps the economy grow.

Young consumers often try to save their money toward a down payment on a house.

Shopping for Savings Accounts

Perhaps you've heard stories of people who stash their savings under floorboards or in mattresses. These people trust no one with their hard-earned cash. Unfortunately, these people are losing out on making money with their savings. By putting their money into a savings account at a bank, they could earn interest. Here is how savings accounts work.

Suppose you put $100 in a bank for one year. The bank says it will pay you 5 percent interest on your money **annually** (yearly). This means that by the end of the year, the bank will have paid you 5 percent of $100, or $5. You would now have $105 in your account. If you decide to open a savings account, it's a good idea to do some comparison shopping. Here are the things to look for:

- *How much interest does the account pay?*

    You can get savings accounts at many different kinds of **financial institutions**. Banks, savings and loans, and credit unions all offer different types of savings accounts with different interest rates. You want to find a high interest rate.

    Obviously, a savings account that offers 8 percent interest is better than one that offers 4 percent interest. But it is also important to know if and how the interest is compounded. In **compound interest** accounts, you earn interest on the interest. Suppose that in the previous example the interest is compounded yearly. The first year you earn $5 interest on $100. You then leave the total of $105 in the account for another year. At the end of that second year, the bank pays you interest on $105 instead of $100. Your interest for the second year will be $5.25. You now have a total of $110.25 in your account.

A regular savings account is often called a *passbook* or *statement* account.

Interest on regular savings accounts is usually compounded monthly or daily. The more often the interest is compounded, the more interest you will earn.

- *Is there a minimum deposit?*

Many times, banks will ask you to keep a certain minimum amount in your savings account. For regular savings accounts, this amount may be as low as $25. In a **money-market account**, the minimum deposit may be as high as $2,500. Money-market accounts usually pay higher interest than regular accounts. And you can often write a limited number of checks on a money-market account. But using a money-market account means you must commit a large sum of money, too.

- *Is it a time-deposit account?*

A **time-deposit account** means that you must leave your money in the account for a certain period of time or you lose interest. For example, one type of time-deposit account is called a **certificate of deposit (CD)**. You buy a CD for a fixed amount of money—$1,000, for example. If you **withdraw** the money before the end of the specified time period, there is usually a penalty. The penalty is often the loss of interest.

These accounts usually earn higher interest than do money-market or regular savings accounts. But you must be prepared to commit a fixed amount of money for a specified time period or you lose interest.

- *Are there any related fees?*

A bank may charge a fee when you open or close certain types of savings accounts. There are often fees for writing checks on savings accounts that allow you to write checks. It is a good idea to know what all the related fees on an account are before you open one.

Comparison of Three Types of Savings Accounts

Type of Account	Advantages	Disadvantages
regular savings account	• you can make deposits and withdrawals whenever you want • low minimum deposit	• usually earns lower interest than other types of accounts
money-market account	• usually pays higher interest than regular savings account • can usually write limited number of checks on the account	• usually requires large minimum deposit
certificate of deposit (CD)	• usually pays higher interest than regular or money-market accounts	• usually requires large minimum deposit for a specified period of time • interest penalty for early withdrawal • you can't make deposits

The advantages and disadvantages of three types of savings accounts are compared in this chart. There are other types of savings accounts in addition to these three. For example, a NOW account is a combination savings and checking account. It pays interest and allows you to write checks. But the interest is lower than on most other savings accounts.

Economics Practice

Use the chart to answer the questions. Write your answers on a separate sheet of paper.

1. What is one advantage of a regular checking account compared to a certificate of deposit?

2. What do money-market accounts require you to do?

3. If you were to start a savings account right now, which would suit you best? Why?

Why Borrow?

Many times, a consumer's savings and income are just not enough. Few people can afford to pay cash for a large purchase such as a home or car. Emergencies may occur that require quick cash. And sometimes, consumers feel they must have new clothes, a stereo, or a meal in a good restaurant. But they may not have the money. When this happens, consumers can borrow money. Usually, this means using a credit card or taking out a bank loan.

When you borrow, you are getting **credit**. You promise to pay back the **principal** (amount borrowed) plus interest over a certain period of time. For example, you might buy a shirt for $50 on your credit card. If you do not pay the $50 (principal) right away, you might be charged 1.5 percent interest on that amount the following month. Instead of owing $50, you now owe $50.75. The longer you wait to pay the principal, the more interest you'll have to pay. As a general rule, consumers look for the lowest interest rate they can find when borrowing.

Credit Cards

Credit cards are very convenient. They are easy to use and handy in emergencies. Quite often, you can even borrow cash and have it charged to your credit card.

Credit cards can be dangerous, too. Because they are so easy to use, people may be tempted to charge up to their credit limit. Then they are left with bills they can't pay. The interest mounts over time, and the consumer loses money.

To keep credit-card costs down, consumers should keep a running total of what they charge each month. This amount should always be within their spending budget.

Consumers should remember that banks and other financial institutions offer credit cards as a service. Most banks consider credit cards a vital part of their business. They make money from the fees and interest that credit-card users pay. Because banks are in competition for credit-card users, consumers can comparison shop for the best deal. Generally, you are looking for cards with the lowest interest and fees. Here are the key things to look for:

Credit cards are also offered by businesses such as department stores and oil companies.

- *What is the annual percentage rate (APR)?*

    This is the total cost of credit expressed as a yearly percentage. It includes the yearly interest that you will be charged on your purchases. It also includes the yearly membership fee, if any. The APR is often as high as 14 or 18 percent. Again, you want to find the lowest APR offered.

- *What are the membership fees?*

    Credit cards often require users to pay a yearly fee.

- *Are there other service or transaction fees?*

Usually, credit-card companies will charge users additional fees for being late on payments, for borrowing cash, or for going over their credit limits.

Bank Loans

Bank loans are not as easy to get as credit cards. They usually require the consumer to fill out many forms. And the consumer must prove that he or she can make the loan payments. Often, banks ask for **collateral**. This is property that the bank will take from you if you fail to make your loan payments.

Bank loans are useful for making large purchases such as homes and cars. Repayment of bank loans can stretch over anywhere from 30 days to 30 years, depending on the type of loan. Just as with credit cards, it is important to shop for the best loan. Once again, look for low interest rates and low service fees. Know as much as you can before you sign on the dotted line.

Economics Practice

Write answers to the following questions on a separate sheet of paper.

1. What is the principal on a loan?

2. If you charge a purchase on a credit card, why is it a good idea to pay it off as soon as possible?

3. What two things should consumers look for when shopping for a bank loan or credit card?

Learn More About It: U.S. Savings Bonds

Another way to save is through U.S. savings bonds. As you learned in Chapter 7, U.S. government bonds are one of the safest investments you can make. You can often buy a bond at less than its face value. You then get the full amount when you cash in the bond at maturity. The bond earns interest until you cash it in.

The most common type of U.S. government bond is the Series EE savings bond. These bonds are available in a range of values from $50 to $10,000. You buy this type of bond for half the amount of the face value. For example, suppose you buy a $100 Series EE government savings bond. You would pay $50. Let's say you have to hold it for eight years until its maturity date. You will earn interest each year at a fixed rate. So when you cash in the bond, you will get the full $100.

Savings bonds have a very important advantage over other types of savings plans. The interest you earn in most regular savings accounts is taxed yearly. It is considered part of your income. But the interest you earn on savings bonds is not taxed until you cash the bond in. People often buy U.S. savings bonds for their children's education. They let the bonds gather interest for many years. They then cash them in when it is time to pay for college tuition. For most people, interest earned on Series EE bonds won't be taxed if the money is used for college tuition.

Chapter Review

Chapter Summary

- Consumers save and borrow to help them pay for large purchases, take care of emergencies, and buy goods and services they want right now.

- It pays to do comparison shopping for savings accounts, credit cards, and bank loans.

- When shopping for a savings account, consumers should look for high-interest accounts with low service fees. Certificates of deposit and money-market accounts may pay higher interest than regular savings accounts. But these accounts often have more restrictions.

- Bank credit cards and bank loans are competitive services offered through banks. Credit cards are also offered by other financial institutions and other types of companies. For this reason, consumers should shop for the best deal. In general, they should look for low interest and low service fees.

Chapter Quiz

Write answers to the following questions on a separate sheet of paper.

A. Thinking About Economics

1. What are two good reasons to save part of your income?

2. How much of your income would you like to be able to save? Why?

3. Why does it make sense for consumers to deposit their savings in a bank instead of keeping it at home?

4. What does it mean when a savings account requires a minimum deposit?

5. What is one advantage of a certificate of deposit as compared to a regular savings account?

6. What is one disadvantage of a money-market account as compared to a regular savings account?

7. What are two things you should look for when choosing a credit card?

8. What is the principal of a loan?

9. What is collateral?

10. Why do you think it is important not to overspend on your credit cards?

B. Personal Economics

Suppose Bank A offers a credit card with an annual percentage rate of 14 percent. Bank B offers a credit card with an annual percentage rate of 18 percent. Bank A charges an annual fee of $75. And Bank B charges no annual fee. Which would you choose? Why?

C. World Economics

The United States is one of the wealthiest nations in the world. But American consumers save less of their income than people in many other countries. One possible reason for such a low rate of savings in this country is that a huge amount of goods and services are available to consumers in the U.S. And through ads, consumers are encouraged to spend their money–either in cash or on credit. Why do you think consumers in Russia save a large part of their income?

Unit Four Review

Write answers to the following questions on a separate sheet of paper.

1. What are three steps a consumer should take in making spending decisions?

2. What is a budget?

3. Why might some consumers prefer to buy generic products rather than name brands?

4. Suppose you wanted to buy a stereo. List at least three ways you could find information about stereos.

5. Why are warranties important?

6. What are two advantages of putting your money into a savings account rather than saving it at home?

7. Why should you shop for different interest rates on savings accounts?

8. Why would you want a credit card with a low annual percentage rate (APR)?

9. What is the difference between the principal and the interest of a loan?

10. Why might a bank ask for collateral when you apply for a loan?

Money and Banking

Chapter 13
Money

Chapter 14
Banking and the Federal Reserve System

Chapter 13

Money

These stones were once used as money on the Pacific Island of Yap. What are some possible problems in using this type of money?

Chapter Learning Objectives

- List three advantages of using money instead of bartering.
- Explain how the use of money helps lead to specialization.
- List five desirable qualities for money, and give examples.
- Define the money supply.

Words to Know

bartering   the direct exchange of one good or service for another without the use of money

counterfeit   illegally reproduced; fake; for example, a *counterfeit* ten-dollar bill

currency   coins and paper money

demand deposit account   a checking account. Funds are payable on *demand* to the holder of the check.

denominations   units of value

durable   lasting a long time without wearing out

money supply   the value of all currency and checking account balances in a country

portable   easily carried or moved

John wanted desperately to move out of his parents' home. He would have to rent a one-bedroom apartment in town. But he didn't have enough money. To solve his problem, he put this ad in the newspaper: *Wanted: room and board in exchange for painting and carpentry. Eager to learn; hard worker.*

Soon John got a call from a young couple who had just bought a big old house. They wanted John to help them fix it up. In exchange, John would get a free room and three meals a day.

For a while, the arrangement worked out well. John painted and did some carpentry work, which he liked. His room was quite small. There wasn't much space for his large collection of books. But he thought he would get used to it. Every evening John ate dinner with the couple. At first he didn't mind. The young man and woman seemed nice enough. The three of them always found things to talk about. But after several weeks of this, John started to feel like he didn't belong there. He longed for more freedom.

John began to think there must be a better way to meet his needs and wants.

Finally John decided he needed a job that would pay him money for his services. If he had money, he'd be able to eat out in restaurants, buy new clothes, and do many other things.

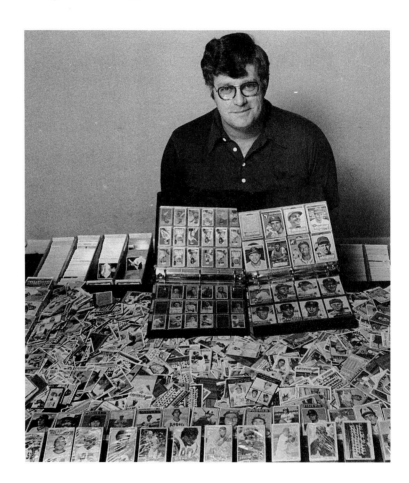

People often barter with baseball cards. Unless the cards have been priced, it's hard to compare the value of one card to another.

Bartering vs. Money

John discovered that bartering didn't work for him. **Bartering** is the direct trade of one good or service for another without the use of money. In this case, John was trading his services directly for shelter and food.

Thousands of years ago, people regularly bartered to meet their needs and wants. Suppose a man caught two fish one day. He might trade one fish to a neighbor for a bunch of berries or a new spear. By bartering, each could share in what the other had.

Like John, these early people found that bartering had its problems. With bartering, each person had to have exactly what the other wanted. What if no one wanted a fish that day? With bartering, it might also be hard to decide just how much of one thing was worth another. Two people might not be able to agree about how many fish were worth one spear.

Another disadvantage was that people could not always save and barter at a later date. The man with the fish had to trade right at that moment for something he wanted. If he saved the fish until next week, he would no doubt be out of luck. The fish would smell so bad no one would want it!

To solve such problems, people came up with the idea of money. Money has three main advantages over bartering. First, money is a widely accepted way to exchange goods and services. That means that most of the time, anyone will accept money in exchange for goods and services. You can use money to buy cars, popcorn, and rubber bands. Any business will gladly accept it.

Have you ever bartered to get something you wanted? What did you trade?

Money can also be used to compare the value of goods and services. Money helps us know what something is worth. If one car is priced at $3,000 and another is priced at $10,000, you know which is worth more. Similarly, if you are offered one job for $5 per hour and another for $7, you know which will buy you more goods and services.

Finally, money is a way to store value. Suppose you earn $20. You can spend it all right away, or you can save it for spending later. You can "trade" the money for goods or services whenever you please.

Now suppose John had put this ad in the paper: *Wanted: painting and carpentry jobs. $12 per hour. Have some good basic skills; willing to learn more. Hard worker.*

Had he taken a job and earned money, he would have avoided many of the problems he found with bartering. He would have known exactly what his labor was worth. He could have traded his wages for almost any goods or services. And he could have saved his money for getting an apartment later.

Economics Practice

Write answers to the following questions on a separate sheet of paper.

1. What is bartering?

2. What is one problem that people often have when they barter?

3. How does the use of money help to solve that problem?

Specialization and Money

There is another important advantage in using money. Money allows people to specialize. What if there were no money? People would be more likely to grow their own food. And they would also make their own shelters and clothing rather than specialize in something like being a math teacher. What if no one wanted to trade food for a math lesson? With the help of money, people are able to specialize and produce more goods and services.

What Are Desirable Qualities for Money?

If you traveled the world, you would find that all money does not look exactly like U.S. money. **Currency** (paper bills and coins) in other countries may be red, black, blue, or purple. Kings, queens, presidents, and other foreign leaders may appear on their countries' coins. And not all countries measure their money in dollars, either. For example, the British use *pounds,* the Nigerians use *naira,* and the Thais use *baht.*

Although these kinds of money may seem different, they are all alike in five important ways:

1. *The money should be widely accepted and recognized.*

    In other words, people will take the money in exchange for goods and services. What is accepted and recognized can vary greatly between cultures and countries. In the United States, for example, people gladly recognize and accept a five-dollar bill. In contrast, people in some African and South American cultures would rather accept cows as money.

2. *The money should be scarce.*

    There must be a limited amount of money, or it loses its value. For example, early Native Americans once used wampum as money. *Wampum* was the name for black and white beads that were used for trading in much the same way we use dollars. The wampum was highly polished and strung in beautiful designs. It took many hours of hard work to make. However, white men soon learned how to make **counterfeit**, or fake, wampum. As wampum became less scarce, it began to lose its value.

To keep money scarce, countries now use special designs, ink, paper, and metals. The more difficult it is to reproduce the money, the harder it is to counterfeit well. In 1991 the U.S. government announced a new way of printing bills. The new bills are threaded with plastic strips that have been coated with metal. Each strip is clearly visible and shows the bill's **denomination**, or value. The strips cannot be reproduced.

3. *The money should be easily divided.*

In some cultures bars of salt were once used as money. The bars were about 12 inches long and 1 ½ inches high. When trading goods and services, people would expertly pinch off just the right amount of salt. Today, most countries have bills and coins of different denominations or values that make it easy to divide and measure money. A dollar bill can be broken into four quarters, a quarter into five nickels, and so forth.

4. *The money should be durable.*

What would happen if people used ice for money? We would have to insulate our wallets and cash registers to keep the money from melting. Otherwise, the money would not last long enough for us to spend it.

Today's money is fairly **durable**. Dollar bills and coins can go through washing machines and dryers and still be usable. Checks may be easily destroyed, but the checking account itself does not disappear.

In ancient China, counterfeiters had their hands or heads cut off as punishment.

If people used ice for money, they would truly be using cold, hard cash!

Most money must be long-lasting and strong to serve its purpose well.

5. *The money should be portable.*

Most of us carry checkbooks, dollars, and coins quite easily in our pockets and purses. This money is **portable**—light and compact. If it were not, it would be hard to carry and use for trading.

In certain cultures, however, portability was not given a high priority. On the Pacific island of Yap, for example, the people used stones as money until World War II. A large hole was carved in the center of each stone. Some of the stones were so large that two people were needed to carry them. Long poles were inserted through the holes. The two people stood on either side of the pole. Then they took a deep breath, picked up the stone, and went on their way!

Today's Money Supply

Currency is produced by two bureaus under the U.S. Department of the Treasury. Coins are produced by the Bureau of the Mint, and paper bills are produced by the Bureau of Engraving and Printing. Together, paper bills and coins make up about ten percent of the money supply. The rest consists of checking-type account balances. Such checking accounts are sometimes called **demand deposit accounts**. This is because banks must provide the account holder with cash right away upon request.

The money supply is an important part of any economy. It can affect prices, loans, jobs, and many other things in your life. You will learn more about how the money supply is controlled in later chapters.

Some economists keep track of how much money is in the economy. Together, currency and checking-type account balances make up one measure of the U.S. money supply. Other measures of the money supply include balances in different time-deposit accounts.

Types of Goods That Were Once Used as Money	
Type of Goods	**Country/Culture**
1. Whales' teeth	Fiji
2. Rats	Easter Island
3. Eggs	Nauru Island
4. Tea	China
5. Salt	Ethiopia
6. Dogs' Teeth	Solomon Islands
7. Snails	Paraguay
8. Stones	Island of Yap

Economics Practice

Use the table to answer these questions. Write answers on a separate sheet of paper.

1. Of the items formerly used as money, which two seem the least portable? Why?

2. Would it be possible to use stones for money in most places? Why or why not?

3. What problems might people have if they used rats for money?

Learn More About It: The $2 Bill

In 1976, the U.S. Treasury Department's Bureau of Engraving and Printing made a fresh batch of $2 bills. The government believed the new currency could be quite useful to consumers. Prices for many goods and services had been rising over the years. And $1 bills were buying less and less.

But Americans took one look at the $2 bill and turned up their noses. People refused to take them from banks or businesses. One bank even tried "selling" the $2 bill for less than $2. They told customers that for $1.95, they could get a crisp, new $2 bill. It did not work.

What was the problem with the $2 bill? No one really knows. The $1 Susan B. Anthony coin, minted in 1979, received the same treatment. People didn't seem to want to use any type of currency that was different from what they were used to. The last Susan B. Anthony coin was minted in 1981.

How would you feel about using a $2 bill?

Chapter Review

Chapter Summary

- Bartering is the direct exchange of goods or services for other goods or services. Bartering can make trading difficult at times. Two people must each have something the other wants. And they must be able to decide on how much their goods or services are worth.

- The use of money makes trading much easier than bartering does. Money is widely accepted by all people in exchange for goods and services. It serves as a way to compare value. And it can be stored or saved for later use.

- For money to be practical, it must be widely accepted and recognized. It also should be scarce, easily divided, durable, and portable. Coins, paper bills, and checking accounts meet those criteria.

- The money supply is often defined as the value of the currency and checking-type account balances in a country. The money supply can affect prices, loans, jobs, and many other things in a person's life.

Chapter Quiz

Write answers to the following questions on a separate sheet of paper.

A. Thinking About Economics

1. Give an example of bartering.

2. What is one disadvantage of bartering?

3. What are the three advantages that money has over bartering?

4. Why does money have to be scarce?

5. Suppose a culture used boulders for money. What is one quality of a boulder that would not be desirable for money?

6. Can a dollar bill be easily divided? Explain.

7. Why should money be portable?

8. Give an example of durable, long-lasting money.

9. How do governments make counterfeiting difficult?

10. What does the U.S. money supply consist of?

B. Personal Economics

As a consumer, do you prefer to use paper money, coins, or checks to pay for goods and services? Give at least two reasons for your choice.

C. World Economics

Millions of people in the developing countries of Latin America, Asia, and Africa live by farming. But many of them produce barely enough food to meet their own needs. And they hardly ever have the opportunity to make money. So they pretty much have to be able to survive without money. What kind of system do you think these people would use for trading goods and services? Explain your answer.

Chapter 14

Banking and the Federal Reserve System

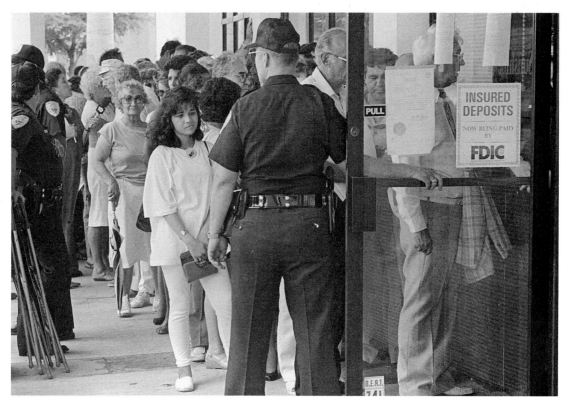

During a bank panic, everyone rushes to withdraw their money at once. The Federal Reserve tries to prevent bank panics from happening.

Chapter Learning Objectives

- Describe what happens during a bank panic.
- Describe the Federal Reserve System and list four things that it does.
- Explain factors to consider when choosing a bank.
- Explain the purpose of the FDIC.

Words to Know

bank panic a situation in which many banks fail because they are not able to meet the demands of their depositors for cash

central bank a bank whose functions include controlling the nation's money supply

check clearing the process in which the Federal Reserve transfers checks and money between banks

commercial banks banks that provide checking accounts and savings accounts, and make loans for a variety of purposes

credit union a kind of bank that is owned by members who belong to a certain company or group

Federal Deposit Insurance Corporation (FDIC) a corporation that insures bank deposits up to $100,000

Federal Reserve System the name of the central bank of the United States

---

The year was 1907. Paul was in town to go to the bank and run some other errands for his family. He needed to buy seeds and fertilizer for their spring crops. Paul planned to withdraw cash from the family's bank account to pay for these things.

When Paul got near the bank, he could see a large crowd. People were waving their arms and shouting. Paul went up to an old man at the back of the crowd.

"What's going on?" Paul asked the man. "What is everybody yelling about?"

"It's a **bank panic**, son," replied the old man. "Everybody is trying to withdraw their money. The bank has run out of cash, so it's closed its doors. We'll probably all lose our savings."

"How can that be?" asked Paul. "My family has money in an account here. I want to take out some of the money that we've deposited. How can the bank run out of money?"

"I've seen lots of bank panics in my time, son," the man said sadly. "You'll be lucky to get any of your money back."

The Federal Reserve System

There were many bank panics in the United States in the 19th century. And they continued to occur in the 20th century. There was a very bad panic in 1907, as shown in the story about Paul. Bank panics happen when people lose confidence in the banks. Everyone rushes to withdraw their money at once.

As Paul discovered, banks do not keep enough cash on hand to pay off everyone at one time. If you deposit $100 in cash in a bank, the bank does not keep all of your $100 there. The bank will keep some of the money and loan out the rest. This system works fine unless everyone wants to withdraw their money at once. In other words, it works fine unless there is a bank panic.

In 1913, the U.S. government decided to do something to try to stop all the bank panics and bank failures. It set up the **Federal Reserve System**. This is the name of the **central bank** of the United States. One of the jobs of the Federal Reserve is to supervise banks to try to prevent them from failing.

The Federal Reserve System is often called "the Fed." Because it is a central bank, the Fed is very different from other banks. The federal government and other banks have accounts with the Fed, but individuals do not. Also, the Fed has the important job of trying to make the economy run smoothly.

The terms "Federal Reserve System," "Federal Reserve Bank," "Federal Reserve," and "Fed" all mean the same thing.

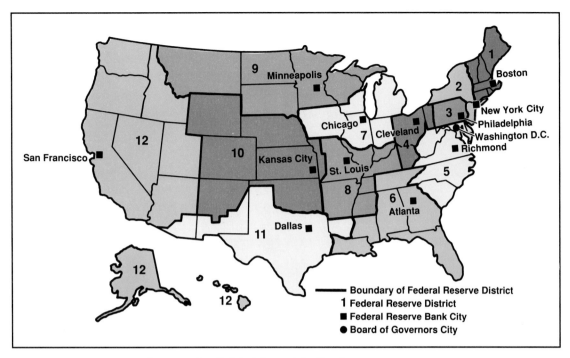

The Federal Reserve System is divided into 12 districts. Each district has a Federal Reserve Bank.

The Federal Reserve System has 12 main banks. As shown in the map, these banks are located in different districts, or in different parts of the country. A committee called the Board of Governors runs the Fed. There are seven people on this important committee.

One thing the Fed does is to try to supervise the nation's banks. It works to make sure that people's deposits are safe so there won't be any bank panics. It sets rules for how much cash banks must keep on hand to back up their deposits.

Another thing the Fed does is called **check clearing**. Suppose Carla lives in Colorado and writes a check for $20 to her cousin Jim, who lives in Wyoming. Jim takes the check to his bank

The chairman of the Board of Governors has been called the second most powerful person in the United States. Who do you think is the *most* powerful person?

and wants to get $20 in cash. Now Jim's bank needs to get the $20 from Carla's bank. Jim's bank sends the check to the Federal Reserve Bank of Denver. The Federal Reserve Bank will transfer the money from Carla's bank to Jim's bank. This is how check clearing works.

The letter and numbers on your dollar bills tell which Federal Reserve Bank distributed them.

The Fed distributes money, but it doesn't print it. Paper money is printed by the U.S. Treasury Department's Bureau of Engraving and Printing in Washington, D.C. Coins are minted in Denver and Philadelphia.

The Federal Reserve Banks issue all of the paper money and coins that are used in the United States. They distribute new dollar bills and collect old, worn-out ones. Look at the picture of the dollar in the photo. (Or, if you have a dollar with you, look at that instead.) Do you see the circle to the left of George Washington's picture? The small print in the circle tells you which Federal Reserve Bank distributed the dollar. The letter L stands for the Federal Reserve Bank of San Francisco . The four number 12s tell you that this is the *twelfth* Federal Reserve District.

The most important thing the Fed does is to try to control the nation's money supply. As you read in Chapter 13, the amount of money flowing through the economy is very important. It can affect prices, interest rates, and even the amount of goods and services produced.

How does the Fed affect the money supply in the economy? It does this by encouraging or discouraging banks from making loans. If people borrow more money, the money supply goes up. If people pay back their loans and borrow less money, the money supply goes down. You will read more about the Fed and money supply in Chapter 21.

Economics Practice

Write answers to the following questions on a separate sheet of paper.

1. What happens during a bank panic?

2. How is a central bank different from other banks?

3. Describe one thing that the Fed does.

Other Types of Banks

The Federal Reserve Bank is the bank for the federal government. People and businesses do not have accounts with the Fed. They bank at places such as commercial banks, savings and loan associations, or credit unions.

Commercial banks provide checking and savings accounts for their customers. They also make loans for things like cars. Until the early 1980s, commercial banks were the only banks that could offer checking accounts. Now other types of banks can offer checking accounts, too.

The major business of savings and loan associations is to make loans to people who want to buy homes. Mutual savings banks also make many home loans. Mutual savings banks are owned by the people who have accounts there. They are located mostly in the northeastern part of the United States.

Credit unions are also owned by the people who do their banking there. Sometimes you must work for a certain company or belong to a certain group to be a member. Credit unions often pay slightly higher interest rates on savings accounts than those paid by other banks. Often they charge lower interest rates on loans, too.

How do you decide where to open a checking account? Where is the best place to save or to borrow? As you read in Chapter 12, it's a good idea to shop around. You can find the best bank the same way you find the best deal on clothes or food.

Here are a few things to consider when you are choosing a bank. If you are going to open a savings account, which bank offers high interest rates? If you are going to take out a loan, which bank charges low interest rates? If you are going to open a checking account, which bank charges low fees? How close is the bank to where you live or work? How friendly and helpful are the people who work there?

Economics Practice

Write answers to the following questions on a separate sheet of paper.

1. What is one difference between a commercial bank and a credit union?

2. List two things to think about when choosing a bank.

3. What is the main type of loan that savings and loan associations make?

Learn More About It: The FDIC

The Federal Deposit Insurance Corporation (FDIC) is not the same as the Federal Reserve System. However, they share an important job—the job of trying to prevent bank panics.

The FDIC was set up in 1934 after many banks failed during the Great Depression. The FDIC insures bank deposits up to $100,000. This means that if a bank fails, the FDIC will pay back people's money, up to $100,000.

This insurance makes people feel secure about having their money in banks. They don't have to worry about losing their money if their bank goes out of business. People will get their money back even if the bank fails. Therefore, they don't rush to withdraw their money.

Most banks have insurance, either from the FDIC or from other agencies. But some do not. In 1985 several savings and loan associations went out of business in Ohio. There was a bank panic, and depositors lost their money. Even today, it is very important to make sure that your bank is insured.

Chapter Review

Chapter Summary

- Bank panics happen when too many people want to withdraw their money at the same time. The Federal Reserve System and the Federal Deposit Insurance Corporation were set up in part to try to prevent bank panics.

- The Federal Reserve (the Fed) is the name of the central bank of the United States. It is run by an important committee called the Board of Governors.

- The Federal Reserve is the bank of the federal government. It supervises other banks, clears checks, and issues money. The most important job of the Fed is to try to control the nation's money supply.

- People and businesses have bank accounts with various kinds of banks. These include commercial banks, savings and loan associations, mutual savings banks, and credit unions.

- It is important to shop around for the bank that best suits your needs.

Chapter Quiz

Write answers to the following questions on a separate sheet of paper.

A. Thinking About Economics

1. Why did the government set up the Federal Reserve System?

2. Which Federal Reserve District do you live in?

3. List three things that the Fed does.

4. What is the most important job of the Fed?

5. Describe how the Fed clears checks.

6. What types of accounts could you have at a commercial bank?

7. Who owns mutual savings banks?

8. Why might you want to join a credit union?

9. What important job do both the Fed and the FDIC have?

10. Why should you make sure that your bank has insurance?

B. Personal Economics

Suppose you are planning to buy a new car. Where will you borrow money to pay for the car? You and the other workers at your company are members of a credit union. Would you apply for a loan through the credit union? Or would you go to a commercial bank? Explain your answer.

C. World Economics

At a commercial bank, it is possible to trade your American dollars for some foreign currency, such as German marks or Mexican pesos. Why might you want to do this?

Unit Five Review

Write answers to the following questions on a separate sheet of paper.

1. What is bartering?

2. Give three reasons why money is often more useful than bartering.

3. What are three qualities that money should have?

4. What is a demand-deposit account?

5. Besides demand-deposit accounts, what else is considered part of the money supply?

6. What is a bank panic?

7. Who can borrow money from the Federal Reserve Bank?

8. What does the Board of Governors do?

9. Who owns credit unions?

10. What kind of insurance does the FDIC provide?

How Well Is the Economy Doing?

Gross Domestic Product

New goods and services are included in the country's Gross Domestic Product (GDP) each year.

Chapter Learning Objectives

- Explain what Gross Domestic Product (GDP) measures.
- Interpret a bar graph showing real GDP.
- Give one reason why GDP may not be a good measure of a country's quality of life.
- Describe what happens during a business cycle.

Words to Know

business cycle   alternating time periods of expanding and contracting economic activity

contraction   a time period when GDP is decreasing

depression   a long-lasting and severe recession

expansion   a time period when GDP is increasing

Gross Domestic Product (GDP) the total dollar value of the final goods and services produced in a country each year

inflation   an increase in the average price of all goods and services

peak   the highest point in the business cycle

real GDP   GDP adjusted up or down to account for inflation

recession   a time period when GDP decreases.

statistics   figures that are collected to get information about a particular subject; numerical data

trough   the lowest point in the business cycle

One night, Felicia was being tutored by her older brother Juan. Juan, a business major, was trying to explain to his sister the importance of economic **statistics**.

"You go to your doctor for a check-up once a year, right?" said Juan. "The doctor takes your temperature, blood pressure, and so forth. The results of these tests help the doctor to determine your overall health."

"Yes," said Felicia. "But what does that have to do with economic statistics?"

"Well, looking at statistics is a way of taking the economy's temperature," said her brother. "Very often, you will hear the economy described as sick, healthy, weak or strong. Such judgments are usually based on these government statistics."

"So," said Felicia thoughtfully, "which statistic is most important?"

"It's difficult to say that one statistic is more important than another. But perhaps the one you will hear the most about is Gross National Product (GNP). Here is where the real lesson begins."

What goods go into this bread that are not final goods?

What Gross Domestic Product Measures

Gross Domestic Product (GDP) measures the total dollar value of the final goods and services produced in a country each year. For example, in 1993 the United States GDP was over six trillion dollars. The bulk of this figure was money spent by consumers on final goods and services.

To understand what is considered a final good or service, think about how bread is produced. First, a farmer grows wheat. A mill buys the wheat and turns it into flour. A bakery buys the flour and makes it into bread. The bakery then sells the bread to consumers. The $1.15 a consumer spends on the loaf of bread is counted in GDP.

This price takes into account the work of the farmer, the miller, the baker, and the seller. The bread is considered a final good because the consumer does not plan to re-sell it to anyone else. GDP does not include the $1.15 for the bread and the price of the flour. By only counting the prices of final goods and services, the government does not count the same product twice.

Economics Practice

Write answers to the following questions on a separate sheet of paper.

1. What does GDP measure?

2. Why is a loaf of bread considered a final good?

3. How does the government avoid counting the same product twice when figuring GDP?

4. Suppose a business buys ink and puts it into its fountain pens. Consumers then buy the fountain pens. Is the ink the final product, or is the pen?

Interpreting GDP

GDP is often used to determine the health of the economy. If GDP has increased from the year before, then production is up. More goods and services are being produced. This usually means that businesses are doing well, more people have jobs, and consumers can spend more.

To accurately judge how much GDP has increased from year to year, the government adjusts it for inflation. **Inflation** occurs when the average price of all goods and services goes up. For example, you may notice that your weekly grocery bill is $5 higher this year than last, although you buy the same foods. This price increase is probably a result of inflation. (You will learn more about inflation in Chapter 16.) If this extra $5 is added to GDP, it will look like more food was produced. In fact, though, prices went up, but nothing extra was produced. Sometimes inflation is taken into account so that only *real* increases in production are measured in GDP. This statistic is called **real GDP**.

GDP is a pretty good measure of what a country produces. But this doesn't mean that it's a good measure of how well off everyone is. For example, a country with a high crime rate may need to spend a good deal on guns and police protection. This would make GDP higher. But people would be better off if there were no crime instead. And a country with serious pollution may have to spend a lot to deal with the problem. Clean-up efforts and enforcement of anti-pollution laws can be very costly. All this spending is added to GDP. But it does not necessarily mean that the country is in good shape, or that people in the country have good lives.

Economics Practice

Use Graph 15.1 to answer the following questions. Write them on a separate sheet of paper.

1. What was the approximate real GDP in 1980?

2. What was the approximate real GDP in 1989?

3. Overall, has production increased or decreased in the United States from 1960 to 1989?

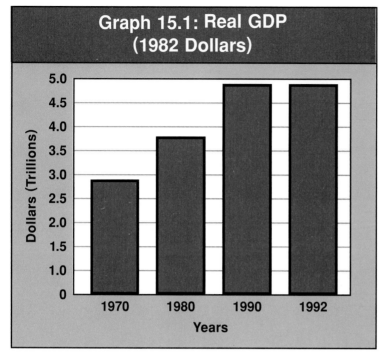

Graph 15.1: Real GDP
(1982 Dollars)

(Source: Department of Commerce, Bureau of Economic Analysis, as reported in the *1994 Information Please Almanac*)

The real GDP of the United States in 1987 dollars

The Ups and Downs of the Business Cycle

As you can see from the graph, GDP in the United States has been increasing. This is an overall trend, however. It does not mean that the economy doesn't catch an occasional cold, flu, or serious illness.

Sometimes production goes up, and sometimes it goes down. This up-and-down economic activity is sometimes called a **business cycle.** When GDP is up, more is produced and more people have jobs. When GDP decreases, less is produced and people lose jobs.

From 1990 to 1991 real GDP decreased. Many people lost their jobs.

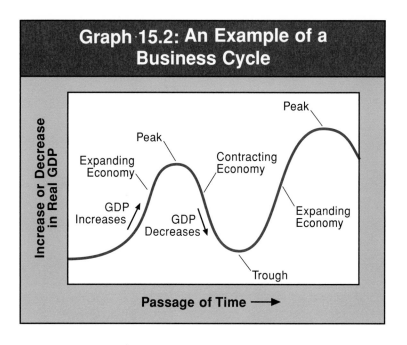

Graph 15.2: An Example of a Business Cycle

Increase or Decrease in Real GDP

Peak

Peak

Expanding Economy

Contracting Economy

GDP Increases

GDP Decreases

Expanding Economy

Trough

Passage of Time →

Graph 15.2 shows an example of a business cycle. During the period of **expansion** or growth in the economy, GDP is increasing. There are new businesses opening, employment is high, and spending is up. At the **peak** period, production is at a high point. But the peak period also marks a turning point.

After the peak period, things begin to slow down. Workers get laid off, and fewer goods and services are produced. This is called the **contraction** of the business cycle. Sometimes this is called a **recession**. During a recession, some businesses decrease production, and others close down completely. This means that jobs are lost, consumers have less to spend, and production decreases even further. If a recession is extremely bad and lasts a long time, it is sometimes called a **depression**.

The National Bureau of Economic Research officially says when a contraction is a recession. Depression usually refers to the time in the 1930's when there were large decreases in output and losses of jobs.

Finally, the economy hits a low point in the business cycle called a **trough**. Then the economy starts to recover and expand. People are hired, and consumers begin to spend again. The cycle starts all over.

It's hard to predict how long a business cycle will last. There is no certain length of time for the economy to go through these up-and-down periods.

There are many opinions as to what causes the ups and downs of the business cycle. The level of business investment and the supply of money and credit play an important role. So does the outlook for future economic activity. And external factors such as the price and availability of oil and the outbreak of war may also play a role.

During the 1970s and early 1980s, there was high inflation *and* high unemployment in the United States. This economic situation is called *stagflation*.

Economics Practice

Write answers to the following questions on a separate sheet of paper.

1. What happens during the expansion period of the business cycle?

2. Describe what happens at a trough in the business cycle.

3. Describe what happens at the peak period of a business cycle.

4. How do we know when the economy is in a recession?

5. What was the severe recession in the 1930's called?

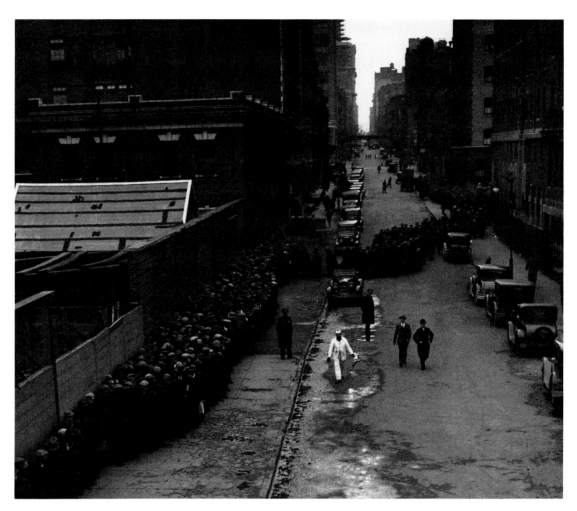

During the Great Depression, almost 25 percent of the labor force could not find work. Breadlines such as this one were a common sight.

The Changing Economic World:
The Great Depression

During the 1920s, many Americans enjoyed great prosperity. Businesses boomed while consumers spent money on radios, cars, clothing, and parties. Many Americans invested in stocks as well, hoping to make an easy profit. But in October of 1929, their hopes disappeared. At that time, many investors tried to sell their stocks all at once. As a result, stock prices fell. Many banks, businesses, and other investors—large and small—were left penniless.

The stock market crash of 1929 was the beginning of a long downturn in the American economy. Between 1930 and 1933, more than 9,000 banks closed their doors and 86,000 businesses failed. Nearly 25 percent of the labor force could not find work. During this period, real GDP fell sharply. This terrible period in United States history is now called the Great Depression.

Chapter Summary

- GDP measures the dollar value of final goods and services produced in a country during a year.

- Increased GDP means higher production, more jobs, and more consumer spending. Decreased GDP means less production, fewer jobs, and less consumer spending. To accurately measure GDP, economists take inflation into account. This statistic is called real GDP.

- Some economists do not believe that GDP is a good measure of quality of life. One reason is because GDP takes into account *all* spending. This includes spending for good things such as education. But it also includes spending for things such as bombs, which some people may find undesirable.

- When GDP goes up and down in a somewhat regular way, this is called a business cycle. During expansions, jobs and consumer spending grow along with GDP. During recessions, jobs and consumer spending decrease along with GDP. The lengths of business cycles vary and are hard to predict.

Chapter Quiz

Write answers to the following questions on a separate sheet of paper.

A. Thinking About Economics

1. Why are economic statistics useful?

2. What does GDP measure?

3. What is the difference between GDP and real GDP?

4. When real GDP is increasing, what happens to jobs and consumer spending?

5. When real GDP is decreasing, what happens to jobs and consumer spending?

6. What is a business cycle?

7. Suppose a graph shows GDP decreasing for two quarters in a row. What does that mean?

8. What is happening to GDP during the expansion period of a business cycle?

9. What is a depression?

10. What is one reason why GDP is not a good measure of quality of life?

B. Personal Economics

When consumers hear that the country may be heading toward a recession, they tend to save more and spend less. Why do you think this happens?

C. World Economics

In 1990, GDP in the United States was almost 6,000 billion (or six trillion) dollars. The population of the United States was about 250 million. So the *per capita* GDP (or GDP per person) was approximately $23,000. In 1992, Indonesia had a population of about 190 million. Yet GDP was only about $122 billion, or about $640 per capita. What do you think these statistics say about the goods and services available for people in Indonesia? How does that compare to the goods and services available for people in the United States?

Chapter 16

Inflation

In 1927, a movie ticket cost 35 cents. How much does it cost to go to the movies today?

Chapter Learning Objectives

- Compare inflation and deflation.
- Interpret the Consumer Price Index (CPI).
- List three effects inflation has on our lives.
- Describe two causes of inflation.

Words to Know

Consumer Price Index (CPI) a statistic used to measure inflation

cost-of-living raise a raise in income to keep wages even with inflation

cost-push inflation the kind of inflation caused by the rising cost of resources such as labor or oil

deflation a decrease in the average price of all goods and services

demand-pull inflation the kind of inflation caused when consumer spending is greater than the amount of goods and services available

fixed incomes incomes that do not change

pension a regular payment to a retired person by his or her former employer

A group of friends stood in line at a movie theater.

"What!" exclaimed Maria. "It costs $7.50 to get in? You're kidding me. The price has gone up a quarter in one month!"

"That's nothing," said Michael. "Popcorn has gone up to $2.50 for the large size. You've got to work for a week just to have a night out."

"Yes, I remember when you could see a movie *and* eat all kinds of stuff for $5," sighed Jeannie.

The friends looked at each other and started to laugh. "We sound like our grandparents," said Maria. She made her voice sound old and scratchy. "Why, I remember when a cup of coffee cost only a nickel, by golly!"

Inflation and Deflation

In the above story, some young friends are having a good laugh at inflation. But most of the time, inflation is no laughing matter. In Chapter 15, you read that inflation is an increase in the average price of all goods and services. But inflation does not necessarily mean that the prices of all goods and services go up equally. Perhaps the cost of entertainment and food rises, while the cost of public transportation goes down. In general, though, inflation means that the average person will pay more for goods and services than before.

The opposite of inflation is deflation. During times of **deflation**, prices go down, on average. This occurred during the Great Depression.

How Is Inflation Measured?

One way to measure inflation is with the **Consumer Price Index (CPI)**. The CPI compares today's prices with the prices of goods and services used by consumers in some earlier year. These goods and services include food, housing, energy, clothing, and so forth.

The CPI is compiled monthly by the Bureau of Labor Statistics. It is regularly announced on the radio and TV news, as well as in the newspapers. Suppose you hear, "The Consumer Price Index rose by 1.3 percent since January." This means that current prices have gone up by 1.3 percent since the beginning of the year.

The CPI is also useful in comparing how prices have changed over time. In the table on page 207, the CPI for the years 1960 through 1993 are listed. The base

Another important statistic is the *Producer Price Index (PPI)*. The PPI is based on changes in prices that producers pay for resources used in producing goods and services.

years are given. Look at any year on the 1982–1984 table—for example, 1975. This means that goods and services that cost you $100.00 in 1982–1984 cost $53.80 in 1975. Prices in 1990 were 30.7 percent higher than in 1982–1984.

The Bureau of Labor Statistics has a CPI Hotline. Anyone can call and find the latest CPI 24 hours per day!

Consumer Price Index for Urban Consumers	
Year	**All Items**
1960	29.6
1970	38.8
1975	53.8
1980	82.4
1982–84	100.0
1990	130.7
1991	136.2
1992	140.3
1993 (March)	143.6

Base Years 1982–1984

(Source: *Monthly Labor Review*, from *1994 Information Please Almanac*)

Economics Practice

Use the table to answer the following questions. Write your answers on a separate sheet of paper.

1. What is the CPI for 1960?

2. By what percentage did 1972 prices rise in comparison to 1982–1984 prices? (Hint: Subtract 100 from the 1992 CPI.)

3. During the 1980s, did the United States experience inflation or deflation? Explain.

The Effects of Inflation

Not many consumers need the CPI to know when there is inflation. The most obvious effect of inflation is that your money doesn't buy as much. Suppose you were working in America in the 1920s, and your annual income was $12,000. You might have been able to buy a new car every year, own a home, and send your children to college. Today, that same $12,000 per year might only get you a small apartment and barely enough food to eat.

Sometimes prices go up gradually. Perhaps you notice that now and then the price of a slice of pizza goes up a dime, or that the bus fare is raised a nickel. But sometimes, inflation can be fast and furious. A severe runaway inflation can do terrible damage to a country's economy. Such a situation developed in Germany in 1923 (see page 210).

Inflation makes it difficult to plan for the future. It's hard to know what the price of a home, car, or college education will be in another 20 years. Tuition has jumped as much as 30 percent in a single year! What could happen to students who saved carefully to get through four years of college at the first-year tuition rate? Such students may find themselves unable to continue.

Inflation especially hurts people with fixed incomes. **Fixed incomes** are incomes that do not change when times change. In today's world, many wages rise with inflation. Workers often get **cost-of-living raises** that keep up with the rate of inflation. But many retired people on **pensions** can't count on raises or bonuses. While prices go up, their incomes stay the same. That means they can buy fewer and fewer goods and services as the years go by. And they can do little about it.

In 1917, a car made by Henry Ford was priced at $360.

What Causes Inflation?

Before inflation can be controlled, it must be understood. What causes it? Economists generally agree that there are two major causes of inflation. The first cause occurs when consumers spend their money faster than businesses can increase production. Of course, people must first *have* the money to be able to spend it. Here is a good example. Suppose that the city of Northville is a highly desirable place to live. It has good schools, there are many jobs nearby, and it is beautiful. Dozens of people want to buy homes there. A few housing developments are under construction. But at the moment there is only one existing home for sale. The asking price is $250,000.

Three people decide to bid on the home. The first person puts in a bid at $250,000. The second person, knowing the scarcity of homes, puts in a bid for $300,000. The third person raises the bid to $325,000. The seller accepts the highest bid, of course. If this same "bidding war" occurred with all goods and services, inflation would soar.

Increases in the money supply lead to inflation.

This type of inflation is called **demand-pull inflation**. It is sometimes decribed as "too many dollars chasing too few goods and services." What if there was plenty of housing for everyone who wanted to live in Northville? Chances are people would not bid more than the asking price of a home.

Inflation can also be caused by the rising cost of important resources. Suppose that the cost of oil goes up. Gas stations make up for this increased cost by raising the price of their gasoline. The price of heating homes and businesses goes up, too. Soon, there is inflation. Inflation caused by the rising price of resources is called **cost-push inflation**.

A little inflation in an economy is often seen as healthy. During times of growth and expansion, more people are working. This means consumers are spending more. When prices go up a little bit, this may encourage businesses to produce more. However, high inflation is not a sign of a healthy economy. In Unit Seven, you will learn more about how the government tries to keep inflation in check.

Learn More About It: Hyperinflation

World War I ended with Germany's defeat. The winning nations demanded that Germany pay them an enormous amount of money to make up for war damages. In 1919, the Treaty of Versailles spelled out how much Germany would have to pay—$33 billion. The payments would have to be spread out over many years. With interest, the payments would add up to $120 billion.

By 1921, Germany was unable to continue making payments and had to borrow huge amounts of money. In 1923 the German government began to print more and more money to keep up with its rising debts. Soon there was so much money in circulation that a very scary runaway inflation was set in motion.

At the beginning of 1923, you could have exchanged four German marks for a dollar. By August of that year, the exchange rate had reached one million marks to the dollar. In December 1923, the exchange rate was 4.2 trillion marks to the dollar!

Try to imagine what life must have been like in Germany that year. The government at one point was printing 46 billion new paper marks each day. People carted their money around in wheelbarrows just to buy a loaf of bread. The money was worth so little that people used it for wallpaper and mattress stuffing. People burned the money for heat. One day the price of a cup of coffee went from 5,000 marks to 8,000 marks in an hour—a 60 percent increase!

The kind of inflation that occurred in Germany in 1923 is called *hyperinflation*.

Chapter Review

Chapter Summary

- Inflation is an increase in the average price of all goods and services. Deflation, the opposite of inflation, is a decrease in the average price of all goods and services.

- The Consumer Price Index (CPI) is one way to measure inflation. It is used to compare the prices of goods and services bought by consumers in some earlier year with today's prices.

- Inflation causes money to lose its value. It makes planning for future spending more difficult. It hurts people whose incomes do not keep up with the price increases. People on fixed incomes, such as the elderly, lose buying power when their dollars lose value.

- Demand-pull inflation occurs when consumer spending increases faster than the available amount of goods and services consumers want to buy. This is sometimes described as "too many dollars chasing too few goods and services."

- Cost-push inflation is caused by the rising cost of important resources. This higher cost is often passed on to consumers in the form of higher-priced consumer goods.

Chapter Quiz

Write answers to the following questions on a separate sheet of paper.

A. Thinking About Economics

1. What is the difference between inflation and deflation?

2. When did deflation occur in the United States?

3. What is the CPI?

4. Suppose the base year for the CPI is 1987. You hear that the CPI for all prices in 1994 is 120. Explain what that means.

5. What is a pension?

6. How does inflation affect people on fixed incomes?

7. Give an example of how inflation may make it difficult to plan for future spending.

8. What does inflation do to the value of the dollar?

9. What is demand-pull inflation?

10. Suppose a labor union wins a wage increase for workers in the auto industry. The auto company passes along this increased cost to consumers by raising the prices of all automobiles. Is this an example of demand-pull or cost-push inflation? Explain.

B. Personal Economics

What is one thing you can do to help live with inflation?

C. World Economics

In 1990, the inflation rate in Brazil was nearly 1,800 percent a year. This compared to an inflation rate of 5.4 percent in the U.S. The Brazilian government came up with a number of anti-inflation programs. But none of them worked. In 1993 prices rose almost 480 percent. So the government has tried to help people cope with inflation by a system of indexing. Wages and interest rates are frequently adjusted to keep up with inflation. Many workers keep getting pay raises month after month. Consumers can earn sky-high interest rates on their savings in banks. So for some Brazilians, inflation doesn't seem all that bad. People have gotten used to it. Some Brazilians even say they *like* inflation. If you lived in Brazil, would you want inflation to continue? Why or why not?

Chapter 17

Unemployment

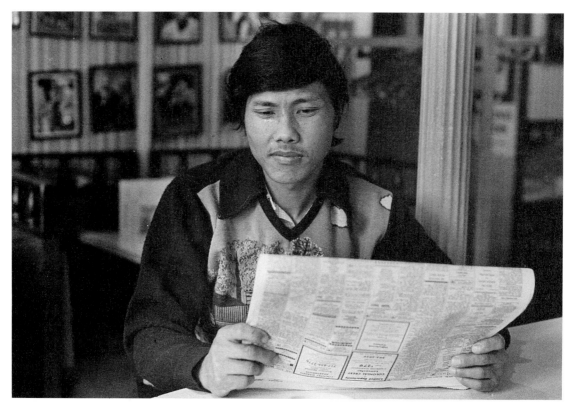

Reading the want ads in a newspaper is one way to look for a new job.

Chapter Learning Objectives

- Define the unemployment rate.
- List four causes of unemployment.
- Explain what full employment means.
- Explain why the unemployment rate may vary among different groups of people.

Words to Know

cyclical unemployment a situation that occurs when people are out of work because of a downturn in the business cycle

frictional unemployment a situation that occurs when people are between jobs or are looking for their first jobs

seasonal unemployment a situation that occurs when people are out of work for a part of the year because of the seasonal nature of their jobs

structural unemployment a situation that occurs when people are out of work because they lack the skills or education necessary for available jobs

unemployment rate the percentage of people in the labor force who are looking for work but have not found jobs

Carol is a 44-year-old welder. She usually works on large construction projects, but was recently laid off. She is now applying for work with many different companies. In the meantime she has put off trading her old car for a new one. And she has decided to wait until next year to buy a new winter coat.

Because Carol is not working, she is not producing goods and services. Imagine what happens to the economy when thousands or even millions of people are out of work. Just think of all the production that is lost.

Unemployment can be a serious problem for those who are out of work and cannot find a job. But it can also become a problem for many others. People who are out of work usually don't spend as much money as people who have jobs. And they certainly tend to put off any major purchases, such as a new car, TV, or washing machine. The many businesses that sell such products suffer.

The Unemployment Rate: How Is It Measured?

In Chapter 9, you learned that the labor force is made up of people 16 years old or older who either have jobs or who are actively looking for work. The United States government defines the *unemployed* as those people who want to work but cannot find a job. Carol fits into this category, because she is actively looking for a job.

The **unemployment rate** is the percentage of people in the labor force who want work but cannot find it. For example, suppose the unemployment rate is 7 percent. That means 7 out of every 100 people in the labor force are not working but are actively looking for jobs.

Many unemployed people have given up looking for work. The government doesn't include these people in its unemployment figures.

U.S. Unemployment Rate	
Year	**Unemployment Rate**
1920	5.2%
1932	23.6%
1944	1.2%
1956	4.1%
1968	3.6%
1976	7.7%
1982	9.7%
1990	5.5%
1993 (April)	7.0%

(Source: Bureau of Labor Statistics as reported in the *1994 Information Please Almanac*)

Economics Practice

Use the table to help answer the following questions. Write your answers on a separate sheet of paper.

1. In 1932, the United States was in the depths of the Great Depression. What was the unemployment rate that year?

2. In 1944, the United States was involved in World War II. There was high production of goods and services related to the war. What was the unemployment rate that year?

3. In 1982, the United States unemployment rate hit its highest point in 40 years. What was the unemployment rate that year?

The Causes of Unemployment

When most people hear that the unemployment rate is rising, they get nervous. Does it mean that the economy is going into a recession? Is it a sign that times will get tough for everyone? It depends. There are four types of unemployment. Some of them are signs of an economic downturn, and others are not.

1. Some unemployment is caused by changes in the business cycle.

You read about this in Chapter 15. When the economy is growing, production is up and GDP is increasing. There are a greater number of jobs. But eventually businesses stop growing. After the business cycle peaks, production begins to shrink or contract. GDP decreases. Businesses may lay off or fire workers to cope with the situation. The unemployment rate may rise. This kind of unemployment is called **cyclical unemployment**.

Remember that a *recession* means that fewer goods and services are produced. This means fewer jobs.

2. Some unemployment is seasonal.

Suppose you are a construction worker in New Hampshire. During the summer, you have plenty of work building homes, working on road construction, and so forth. But when the wintry weather comes, you often find yourself unemployed along with many of your co-workers. Farm workers, landscapers, and lifeguards may also find themselves seasonally unemployed.

Workers who experience **seasonal unemployment** may try to save enough to get by during the off season. Or they may try to plan dual careers. For example, the summer gardener may try to get an indoor job in the winter. The gardener might work as a science teacher's aide. Likewise, a person who works on snow removal in the winter may try to get a summer job as a gardener.

Seasonal unemployment may cause a temporary rise in the unemployment rate. But it does not necessarily mean that the whole economy is in a downturn or heading for a recession.

3. Some people are unemployed because they lack the skills or education to find jobs.

In Chapter 9, you read how automation can affect workers in a certain industry. Many Detroit auto workers have been displaced by electronic robots that now do their work. These workers may have trouble finding new jobs because they lack the right experience, skills, and education.

Unemployment caused by lack of skills is called **structural unemployment**. It may hit different industries at different times. This type of unemployment can often be lowered through further education and training when it is available. For example, more and more unions are offering job retraining programs for workers who've lost their jobs. This job retraining helps the workers to cope with new job requirements. The workers are taught the new skills they will need to know.

4. *Unemployment can be caused when people voluntarily quit to find new jobs.*

Suppose you have a job as a secretary. To get to the office, you have to drive 30 miles to work each day. So when your car breaks down, you quit your job and look for something closer to home. In the meantime, you are added to the unemployment rate. Any other people in the same situation are added, as well.

This type of unemployment is called **frictional unemployment**. It doesn't mean that the economy is in bad shape. It means that workers have the freedom to quit jobs to look for better ones.

This worker may become one of the seasonally unemployed.

Economics Practice

Write answers to the following questions on a separate sheet of paper.

1. What is one example of seasonal unemployment?

2. What happens to the unemployment rate during a recession?

3. What is one example of structural unemployment?

Full Employment

A goal of most governments is to have enough jobs for everybody who wants to work. This doesn't mean that there should be *no* unemployment, however. Why not? Remember what the situation is like in a free market economy such as that of the United States. People are able to choose their jobs, careers, and places of employment. In a free society, there will always be some unemployment caused by people quitting their jobs and looking for new ones.

It is probably unrealistic to think that any country could fully eliminate other causes of unemployment as well. However, it is a government goal that temporarily unemployed people should find work reasonably quickly.

Unemployment Among Different Groups

In April 1993, the unemployment rate in the United States was 7 percent. This means that out of every 100 people in the labor force who were willing to work, 93 had jobs. Yet you may know many people in your area who are unemployed. There may seem to be far more unemployment than you might expect from this national figure. How can that be?

The national unemployment figure looks at the total labor force throughout the United States. Suppose you divided the labor force into various groups. You would find that the unemployment rate varies by industry, state, city, age, and race. For example, the unemployment rate in Albuquerque, New Mexico, was 4.6 percent in 1993. This is a booming "sunbelt" city where many jobs are available. On the other hand, the unemployment rate in Detroit was 16.5 percent that same year. This higher rate was partially due to changes in the auto industry.

The young and minorities are the two groups often hit hardest by unemployment. The young often lack the necessary experience, skills, and education to get good jobs. Few 16-year-olds will get jobs as computer engineers, for example. But there may be a great number of these positions available. Often, jobs that the young are qualified to do may be difficult to get. That's because so many people want these jobs. During the summer, there may be hundreds of applicants for fast-food restaurant jobs, for example. Yet there are only a few openings. And many times, these jobs do not pay much.

Minorities often experience high unemployment, too. Sometimes this is due to lack of education and skills. For example, new immigrants to this country may lack the necessary language skills to get jobs. In addition, minorities have often had fewer opportunities to get a higher education. This can sometimes make it difficult to find employment.

Some of the high unemployment among minorities may be due to prejudice, as well. Employers may prefer to hire whites over minorities, even though the minority applicants have the same or better qualifications. Improved enforcement of civil rights laws and affirmative action programs has improved this situation somewhat in recent years. However, there are still great strides to be made in this area.

In 1992, the rate of unemployment for minority men ages 16 to 19 was 21.5 percent. For white male workers 20 years or older, it was 6.3 percent.

Economics Practice

Write answers to the following questions on a separate sheet of paper.

1. Which two groups are often hit the hardest by unemployment?

2. Why doesn't the United States strive for a zero unemployment rate?

3. Give one reason why the unemployment rate may be high in one city and low in another.

Franklin Delano Roosevelt (1882–1945)

What It Means to Me: Unemployment Insurance

In the 1930s, during the Great Depression, United States unemployment soared to a record 23.6 percent. Under the leadership of President Franklin D. Roosevelt, many relief programs were started to help the jobless. One of the most important of these was *unemployment insurance.*

Most states started unemployment insurance progams in 1938 and 1939. Under these programs, employers pay a certain amount of taxes into their state's unemployment fund. Then the fund pays workers a temporary income if they're laid off. Not all workers who lose their jobs are eligible for these benefits. For example, a worker who had been fired for often being late probably would not get any unemployment benefits. Most workers who voluntarily quit their jobs are not eligible, either.

Workers who qualify usually receive unemployment benefits based on a percentage of their previous wages. In most states, unemployed workers receive payments every two weeks for a maximum 26 weeks. In times when unemployment is especially high, payments are often extended for another 26 weeks. During this period, unemployed workers must register for work with the state employment agency. And they must accept any suitable jobs they're offered. If they do not, the unemployment benefits are stopped.

Unemployment programs vary from state to state. To find out more about them, ask the employment department in your area.

Chapter Review

Chapter Summary

- The unemployment rate is the percentage of people in the labor force who are actively looking for work and cannot find it.

- There are four types of unemployment. *Cyclical* unemployment is caused by contraction in the business cycle. Some unemployment is *seasonal*. *Structural* unemployment is the result of workers not having the necessary job skills and education. And *frictional* unemployment is caused by workers who voluntarily quit their jobs and look for new ones.

- Some unemployment will always exist in a free market economy. People may be temporarily unemployed when they change jobs.

- The unemployment rate varies among industries, cities, states, and population groups. Unemployment is typically higher among the young and minorities than in other groups. Part of this may be due to lack of education, experience, and skills. Prejudice may also account for some of this difference.

Chapter Quiz

Write answers to the following questions on a separate sheet of paper.

A. Thinking About Economics

1. What is meant by the unemployment rate?

2. Suppose the country is in a recession. How will this affect unemployment?

3. Give an example of seasonal unemployment.

4. Give an example of structural unemployment.

5. Suppose a woman quits her job to have a baby. She does not look for a new job. Is she counted in the unemployment rate?

6. Suppose a man quits his job as a hotel clerk and looks for a job at another hotel. Is he counted in the unemployment rate?

7. Why will some unemployment always exist in a free market economy?

8. The unemployment rate among young people is often higher than the unemployment rate for the entire nation. Give one possible reason for this.

9. The unemployment rate among minorities is often higher than the unemployment rate for the entire nation. Give one possible reason for this.

10. When is a worker eligible for unemployment benefits?

B. Personal Economics

How can education and job training help keep you from being unemployed?

C. World Economics

1. In 1989, the unemployment rate in the U.S. was 5.3 percent, while in Mexico it was 20 percent. Why do you think many Mexicans chose to go north to the U.S. to look for work?

2. In 1990, Japan had a problem that was the opposite of unemployment. There was a growing labor *shortage*. There were three jobs available for every Japanese worker who was seeking a job! Companies had to offer higher wages and better non-wage benefits in order to attract and keep workers. As a worker in Japan, would you have been pleased with this situation? Why or why not? In spite of the labor shortage, do you think that there was any unemployment in Japan? If so, what type of unemployment would you find there? Explain.

Chapter 18

The Problem of Poverty

Public and private programs provide aid to the poor.

Chapter Learning Objectives

- Explain how poverty is measured in the United States.
- Describe four things that could affect a person's standard of living.
- Explain how income is transferred to the poor.
- Describe social insurance and social welfare programs.

Words to Know

charities   non-profit organizations that accept donations such as money, goods, and volunteer time, and then provide aid to needy people

poverty line   the minimum yearly income that a family must have in order to meet its basic needs

social insurance programs   a variety of programs meant to prevent poverty. Social Security, worker's compensation, unemployment insurance, and Medicare are well-known examples. Workers pay into these programs while they are employed.

social welfare programs   programs that provide income, housing, and health insurance to the individuals and families who cannot work

---

The War on Poverty

In 1962, Michael Harrington wrote a book called *The Other America*. In it, he described the terrible situation of America's poor. He said they lived in the country and in the cities; they were white, black, young, and old. At that same time, minorities began to cry out for equal economic opportunity. They wanted equal education, equal jobs, and equal pay. It seemed that while many Americans were prospering, others were being left behind.

As a result, President Lyndon Johnson later declared a "war on poverty." The government armed itself with tax dollars. It began to spend billions of dollars on   new programs to help the poor.

Now, about 30 years later, 14.2 percent of Americans still live in poverty. This figure is down from 18.1 percent in 1960. And while many people agree that the war is not over, few people agree on how to win it. This chapter looks at the problem of poverty and how it is handled in the American economy.

How to Measure Poverty

In 1964, the Social Security Administration established the **poverty line** as a system of measuring poverty. The poverty line is also called *poverty level* or the *poverty threshold*. The poverty line is the minimum yearly income that a family must have in order to meet its basic needs. Any family earning below that amount in the United States is living in poverty. For example, the poverty level for a family of four in 1989 was $12,675. The government estimated that one-third of this amount was required to meet basic food needs. The other two-thirds would take care of shelter, clothing, and medical needs. Any family of four who received less than that amount of income was counted as living in poverty.

The U.S. government has established poverty lines for families of one to nine persons. The figures are adjusted each year for inflation based on the Consumer Price Index. The table shows how the poverty line has changed in the last 20 years.

Remember that inflation means prices are going up. So it costs more to buy food, clothing, and so forth in 1990 than it did in 1970.

Poverty Lines in the United States			
Family Size	**1970**	**1980**	**1991**
1	$1,954	$4,190	$6,932
2	$2,525	$5,353	$8,865
4	$3,968	$8,414	$13,924
6	$5,260	$11,269	$18,587

(Source: U.S. Bureau of the Census as reported in *1994 The World Almanac and Book of Facts*)

Economics Practice

Use the table to help answer the following questions. Write your answers on a separate sheet of paper.

1. What does the poverty line mean?

2. What was the poverty line for a family of four in 1970? In 1990?

3. Why are the figures so different? Explain.

Poverty and the Standard of Living

Some people do not believe that the poverty line accurately measures a person's standard of living. In other words, a person's income may not really measure how well he or she lives. For example, suppose that Joe Smith inherited a nice home and $100,000. He puts the cash in a savings account where he earns 5 percent interest annually. Each year, he earns about $5,000 in interest. Joe's needs are simple. He doesn't have a job. But he easily pays for his food, clothing, health insurance, and taxes. Yet, his income puts him below the poverty line.

On the other hand, the Andersons, a family of six, earn $19,000 a year. They are considered to be living above the poverty line. But Mr. and Mrs. Anderson are raising four children. They have a constant struggle trying to make ends meet.

Another thing to consider is where a person lives. The cost of living may vary greatly in different parts of the country. Heating bills in New York City will be much higher than in Daytona Beach, Florida. Housing may be more expensive in Los Angeles than in Kansas City. Thus, a family may live better on $12,000 in one city than in another. Yet, the poverty threshold is the same in either city.

Many people believe that it is important to take the following factors into account when determining poverty: Does a person own property, such as a house or car? Does the person receive food stamps or government-provided health insurance? How much tax does the person pay on his or her income? Where does the person live? All of these things will determine how well-off a person is. But to accurately measure the standard of living for each family would be too complicated. Therefore the government has continued to classify people as poor only if they fall below the nationwide poverty line.

Economics Practice

Write answers to the following questions on a separate sheet of paper.

1. What is meant by a person's standard of living?

2. Besides income, what are three things that might affect a person's standard of living?

Charitable organizations such as the Red Cross distribute aid to disaster victims.

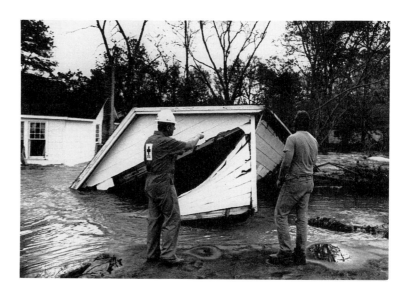

The Transfer of Income

In most societies, some attempt is made to deal with the problem of poverty. Income must be transferred from those who have it to those who do not. Suppose you earn ten dollars each week and your friend earns nothing. To help your friend out, you give him five dollars. You are transferring some of your income to your friend.

In the United States, this transfer of income happens through charities and through the government. **Charities** are non-profit organizations that accept donations such as money, goods, and volunteers' time. They then distribute aid to people in need. Charities may set up meal services, homeless shelters, medical-aid funds, and so forth.

Some large charitable organizations work on a national and even an international level. For example, the Red Cross provides emergency housing and medical care. This help is offered when there is a natural disaster such as a hurricane or an earthquake. The United Way is another well-known organization. It distributes its funds to hundreds of smaller charities. Many other charitable programs are run by churches, local clubs, and small businesses in a community. There are thousands of important charitable organizations throughout the country.

Major corporations may sponsor charitable programs as well. For example, some businesses have begun helping schools. They may donate computers, share knowledge of the business world, and provide job training to students. Many business people believe these contributions will better prepare tomorrow's workforce. Workers with more education have more skills and are more productive. This will help to keep American businesses competitive with foreign businesses.

Name a charity in your own community.

A philanthropist is a person who loves humankind and shows this love through charitable acts.

Government Programs

Income is also transferred through the federal, state, and local governments. Citizens pay their taxes to these governments. The governments then distribute some of these tax dollars to people in need through various programs. Most programs dealing with poverty are run at the state level. But it is important to remember that many state programs depend on federal funding. And many local programs may depend in part on state funding. Federal laws and guidelines may influence these programs as well.

Government programs can be divided into two major groups. **Social insurance programs** were started during the Great Depression with the passage of the Social Security Act of 1935. These programs provide regular income and health insurance. Those eligible include the elderly, the disabled, the unemployed, and sometimes family members who survive a parent's death. The people who are eligible to receive these benefits have usually contributed directly to the programs in tax dollars. They pay into these programs while they are employed. For example, suppose Jill Smith is a teller at a bank. Social Security taxes are taken regularly from her paycheck for 25 years. Her employer pays an equal amount of tax into the fund for her each pay period. When Jill reaches age 62, she can retire and get Social Security benefits. The amount she gets will depend on what she and her employers have contributed over Jill's life. If Jill dies, her children may be entitled to some of her benefits.

The Social Security program is run by the federal government. It provides income and medical benefits for those retired or unable to work. It is one of the largest social insurance programs in the country.

Why do you think government social insurance programs were started during the Great Depression?

State-run social insurance programs include unemployment insurance (see Chapter 17), worker's compensation, and Medicare. Under the worker's compensation program, a person hurt on the job is entitled to medical benefits. If the person dies, his or her family may be entitled to some money. Medicare is a health insurance program for the elderly and disabled.

Social insurance programs were started to prevent poverty. Unfortunately, the benefits from these programs have not always kept up with the cost of living. As a result, even those who receive such benefits may sink below the poverty line.

Social welfare programs provide income, housing, and health insurance to poor individuals and families. These are people who for various reasons cannot work to make a living. Funding for these programs comes from tax dollars. For example, Aid for Families with Dependent Children (AFDC) provides money to families in need. Such families often receive additional help. They may get food stamps and a type of health insurance called Medicaid. Social welfare may also go to the handicapped, disabled veterans, and others who cannot work.

In recent years, many social welfare programs have come under attack. Critics say that welfare supports the poor, but doesn't help them escape poverty. In addition, many of these programs have experienced large budget cuts. Some social welfare programs now require those who receive benefits to get job training or do community work. The idea is to teach new job skills. This will help welfare recipients get jobs and earn a decent income. Some people see this as a more efficient use of tax dollars. They believe the money is better spent on training people for jobs rather than simply providing welfare.

Unmarried women with children are far more likely to be on welfare and in poverty than other women. In the United States, about 40 percent of single-parent families are headed by women who are in poverty.

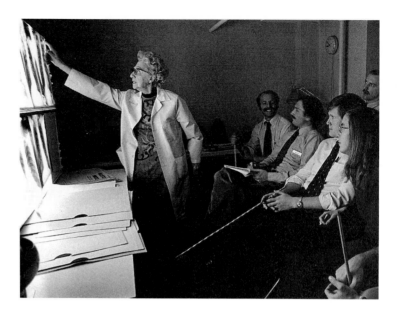

Many elderly people depend on Social Security benefits when they retire.

Economics Practice

Write answers to the following questions on a separate sheet of paper.

1. Describe one social insurance program.

2. Give one reason why social insurance programs do not always prevent poverty.

3. Describe one social welfare program.

4. Why are some social welfare programs now requiring people to get job training?

5. What is Medicare?

6. Why do some people feel that welfare is not a good idea?

The homeless are a growing segment of the U.S. population.

Learn More About It: The Very Poor

Imagine yourself a single mother with two children. Each month you get less than $200 and some food stamps from the state. Home is a run-down apartment where the gas and water leak. To make ends meet, you gather aluminum cans and glass, then sell them to be recycled. Often, you and your children are hungry and cold.

You are one of America's very poor. The very poor are those who live on less than half of the poverty line income. In 1989, one out of 20 Americans fit into this category. Among the very poor are an increasing number of homeless people. These people live in parks, on city streets, in their cars, or in homeless shelters. Some of the homeless actually have jobs, but they don't earn enough to rent a room. In New York City, large numbers of homeless men, women, and children live in the subway tunnels. They have sometimes been called "mole people" because they live underground like moles.

Most very poor families (61 percent) are headed by single mothers. The families include about 4.9 million children. Two out of five of the very poor receive some kind of welfare from the government.

The very poor population increased by 45 percent from 1979 to 1989. Some economists and government officials blame this on cuts in welfare spending. Others blame drugs, the high dropout rate, and teenage pregnancy. No one is sure what is causing this increase.

Even more perplexing is the solution. Government officials are sure that simply pumping money into social programs is not the answer. But they have yet to come up with a better solution. What are your ideas?

Chapter Review

Chapter Summary

- Eliminating poverty has been a major economic goal of the United States since the 1960s. The government has established poverty lines. These specify the minimum yearly income a family must have in order to meet its basic needs. Those who fall below that level are considered to be in poverty. But poverty lines do not take certain things into account. These include personal property, other types of government aid, taxes, or cost of living in certain areas. Poverty lines are not always considered a good measure of standard of living.

- To help ease poverty, income is transferred to the poor through private charities and the government. Private charities use donations to provide meal services, shelters, medical funds, and so forth. The government uses tax dollars to aid the poor in many different ways.

- In 1935, the government set up a system of social insurance programs. These programs provide income and medical care to the elderly, the unemployed, the disabled, and their survivors. These programs are mainly funded by tax contributions of employers and their employees. The workers pay into the programs while they are employed. These programs were meant to prevent poverty. The benefits they provide do not always keep a person above the poverty line, however.

- Social welfare programs provide income, medical care, food, and shelter to poor people who cannot work. This includes families with single mothers and handicapped people in need. In recent years, funding for these programs has been cut. More and more of these programs are emphasizing job training and education to help people escape poverty.

Chapter Quiz

Write answers to the following questions on a separate sheet of paper.

A. Thinking About Economics

1. Who declared the "war on poverty" in the 1960s?

2. What is a poverty line?

3. List three other factors besides income that could be used to determine a person's standard of living.

4. How do charities transfer income to the poor?

5. Give an example of a private charity and explain what it does.

6. How do governments transfer income to the poor?

7. What group of programs were started by the Social Security Act of 1935?

8. Why don't social insurance programs always prevent poverty?

9. What do social welfare programs do? Give an example.

10. What is one way social welfare programs have changed in recent years?

B. Personal Economics

What are two things you can do to ensure that you have a good standard of living?

C. World Economics

Poverty is a problem in the United States even though the United States is the richest nation on earth. But poverty is much more severe and widespread in many other parts of the world. The United Nations Children's Fund (UNICEF) provides aid for children in need, job training, and family planning in many countries. While some of UNICEF's funding comes from private donations, most comes from governments. The money contributed by the U.S. government comes from American taxpayers. Do you think that American taxpayers should provide help for the poor in other countries? Why or why not?

Unit Six Review

Write answers to the following questions on a separate sheet of paper.

1. What statistic measures the dollar value of final goods and services produced in a country during a year?

2. How does GDP change when we are in a recession?

3. When the economy is expanding, what is happening to production and jobs?

4. What does the CPI measure?

5. How does inflation affect the amount of goods and services your money can buy?

6. One type of inflation is caused when consumer spending goes up faster than the available amount of goods and services. Another type of inflation is caused by the rising cost of resources. Give an example of this second type of inflation.

7. What does the unemployment rate measure?

8. Why will some unemployment always exist in a free market economy?

9. How does the United States government measure poverty?

10. What are two ways that income is transferred to the poor in the United States?

Unit Seven

Government and the Economy

Chapter 19

The Role of Government in a Free Market Economy

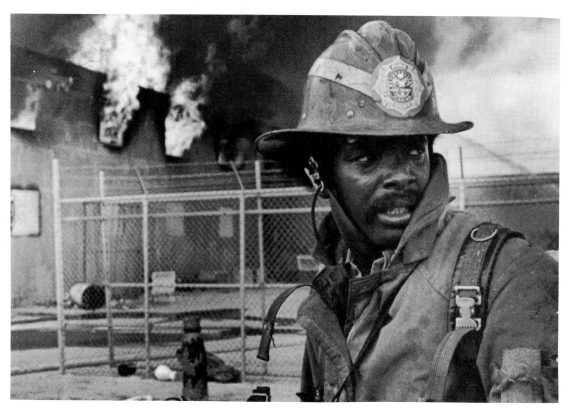

Fire and police departments are among the goods and services provided by the government.

Chapter Learning Objectives

- Describe three goods or services the government provides.
- Describe three ways the government regulates economic activity.
- Explain how the government uses taxes to provide goods and services.

Words to Know

estate tax   a tax on the property of a person who has died

excise tax   a tax on certain items such as alcohol, tobacco, and gasoline

income tax   a tax individuals pay on income above a certain amount and corporations pay on profits

inheritance tax   a tax on inherited property or money

laissez faire   a basic policy that calls for non-interference by the government in business matters

sales tax   a tax on purchases

What's the Connection?

It is a typical day in the American city of Youngston. Rick is a reporter working on a special story. He walks around and records the sights and sounds of the city. These are his notes:

- An ugly car accident happens at Eighth and Main streets. Police arrive at the scene to take reports and direct traffic. An ambulance rushes the driver to a hospital's emergency room. Onlookers stare in silence.

- The mayor gives a speech at a new building development downtown. She claims it will bring jobs and help the city's economy. The city government had agreed to pay part of the building costs. This was the best way to get the builder interested in the project. Workers on their lunch hour clap politely amid the red, white, and blue ribbons that stream around the construction site.

- A tenth-grade gym class gathers on the playing field at Youngston High. They put on their baseball gloves and begin spring practice.

What could Rick's story be about? He is going to write about the government services that the public uses, and the taxes the public pays to get them. He is going to write about the role of government in a free market economy.

The Government's Role

To review the characteristics of a free market system, look back at Chapter 2.

In Chapter 2, you read about the characteristics of a free market system. In a free market system, it is mainly individuals who decide what goods should be produced, how they should be produced, and who will get them. Businesses and consumers play important roles in this type of economy.

But in the United States' free market economy, the government plays a role, too. In this chapter, you will read about some important goods and services the government provides. You will also read about taxes and how they are used.

Government Goods and Services

Suppose for a moment that you had the same assignment as Rick the reporter. Your job is to notice the various goods and services that the government provides. What might you write about?

It is likely that you would write about the public schools in your city. You might also write about the police and fire departments. The public parks, the sewer system, street and traffic lights, public health services, jails, and so forth are all provided by the government. There are hundreds if not thousands of services to write about.

Think of one government service that you have used this week.

There are three levels of government which provide these goods and services. For example, the federal government runs the army, navy, and all military departments. State governments provide some of the

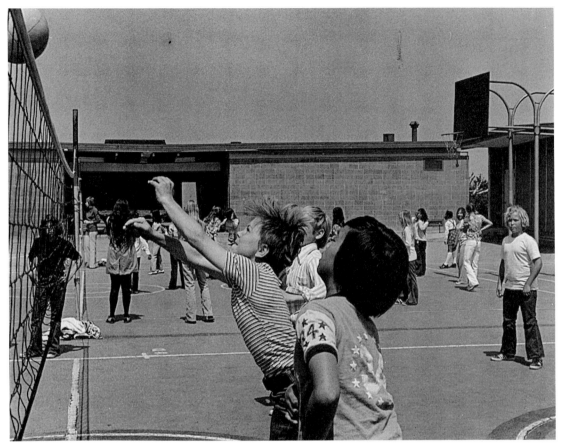

Public schools are paid for by tax revenues.

funds for roads, schools, and courts. At the local level, both county and city governments may provide police and fire protection.

Why does the government provide these services in a free market economy? Why not let private businesses provide these things? Suppose for a minute that providing armed forces was not a service offered by the government. Instead, this service would have to be provided by a private business. Clearly, it would be very expensive to provide a trained army, navy, air force, and so forth.

How would a private business charge people for this service? This would be a big problem, because private businesses cannot collect taxes. They would have to ask people to donate money. Some people probably would give money. Other people might say, "Why should I contribute? If the country can be protected by using other people's money, then I am protected, too." So what would happen? It would be difficult to raise money from everyone. Therefore it is likely that the armed services would be small if it were left to a private business. This is one reason why the government steps in.

In the United States, all citizens are guaranteed certain rights by the Constitution. They have the right to own private property and the right to a speedy trial. The government provides a system of courts and jails to protect people's rights to private property. These rights might not always be guaranteed if it were up to private businesses to protect them. Instead, it is up to the government to do so.

The government has another function in a free market economy. It provides a system of courts and jails to protect people's rights to private property.

Economics Practice

Write the answers to the following questions on a separate sheet of paper.

1. What three levels of government provide goods and services?

2. Give an example of a service that is provided at the local level.

3. What might happen if the government did not provide public schools?

Regulating Economic Activity

Some economists believe that a true free market economy should have a policy of **laissez faire**. This French term means that the government should not interfere in matters of business. The economy should by left to run itself.

In its early years, the United States followed a basic policy of laissez faire. But over the years, it began to establish laws requiring businesses to do certain things. For example, it outlawed monopolies, except when they are regulated by the government, as in the case of utilities. The purpose of this regulation was to help keep competition strong in America. Also, the government requires businesses to produce reliable and safe products and services. This type of regulation is meant to protect consumers. The government also regulates employment practices, strikes, and other labor/management issues. Again, the purpose of such laws is to protect workers, businesses, and consumers.

The United States also regulates some of the negative effects of economic activity. A good example of this is pollution. Pollution is often caused by the production of steel, plastics, energy, and so forth. Pollution of the air, water, and land may then result in environmental disaster and health hazards. Clean-up efforts and new equipment to prevent pollution are often costly. So it is unlikely that businesses would regulate themselves. As a result, the government takes on this task.

At the federal level, the Environmental Protection Agency (EPA) studies environmental problems and helps regulate pollution. It may fine businesses that do not comply with pollution laws. States and cities may set their own pollution standards as well. In California, for example, smog-control standards for cars are much stricter than in the rest of the country. Cars must pass state smog inspections every two years in order to be registered.

Regulate means to control according to a rule.

In 1989, 81 U.S. cities did not meet government mandated standards for air quality.

Economics Practice

Write answers to the following questions on a separate sheet of paper.

1. What does *laissez faire* mean?

2. Give one example of a negative effect of economic activity.

3. Why should the government try to regulate this negative effect?

Who Pays Taxes?

There is an old saying: There's no such thing as a free lunch. Many government goods and services, such as roads, fire protection, national defense, and pollution regulation, may seem to be free. But these things must be paid for. One of the ways the government gets money to pay for them is through taxes.

Some taxes are paid only by those who will use the corresponding goods and services. For example, most people pay Social Security taxes when they work. This qualifies them to collect Social Security benefits when they retire. Another example is gasoline taxes, which pay for many highway and bridge projects. The drivers who pay these taxes will benefit from those projects.

Other government goods and services are paid for by all tax payers, whether they use them or not. In most cities, for example, all property owners must pay property taxes. Part of this money goes toward public schools. It doesn't matter whether or not the property owners have children in school. The reason behind this is that everyone will benefit by having a more educated population. Likewise, some part of city taxes goes toward parks and civic parades, whether the tax payers use and enjoy these benefits or not. The parades and parks are available to all, although not everyone chooses to enjoy them.

There are many kinds of taxes. People who earn more than a certain amount must pay personal **income tax** to the federal government and often to their state government. Corporations must pay income tax on their profits. And almost all states have a **sales tax**, which requires consumers to pay a tax on certain purchases.

The first United States income tax law was passed in 1862 to help pay for the Civil War.

Type of Tax	Who Pays It?
Corporate income tax	Corporations pay taxes on profits to the federal government and to some state and local governments.
Excise tax	Consumers pay extra tax on certain types of goods such as alcohol, tobacco, and gasoline. These are usually federal taxes, but states can require them as well.
Estate tax	The federal government requires a tax on the property of a person who has died. Some states require it as well.
Inheritance tax	A person who inherits property must pay a state tax on it. Not all states have this tax.
Sales tax	Consumers pay tax on certain purchases. Most state governments have such a tax. The percentage of the tax varies.
Social-insurance tax	Employees and employers pay this tax to the federal government. It is sometimes referred to as FICA

	(Federal Insurance Contributions Act). It pays for Social Security benefits and other social insurance programs.
Personal income tax	Individuals who earn above a certain amount must pay taxes on their income to the federal government. Some states and a few cities require personal income taxes as well.
Property tax	Property owners must pay taxes on land, homes, and other owned property to most state and local governments.

Economics Practice

Write answers to the following questions on a separate sheet of paper. Use the table for help.

1. Who has to pay a sales tax?

2. What kinds of goods have an excise tax?

3. If you inherit a home, what type of taxes might you have to pay?

How Involved Should the Government Be?

Samuel Salter is a small-business owner. He wishes he didn't have to pay so much money for taxes and for things such as business licenses. He believes he could better use this money to help his business grow. He thinks that the government plays too big a role in the United States' free market economy.

Karen Hicks is also a small-business owner. She doesn't like all the taxes she must pay, either. But she appreciates many of the government services she gets for them. For example, she has received lots of good information from the Small Business Administration (SBA) to help her business succeed. She believes the government should do whatever it can to improve business in her community and the country as a whole. She would not mind at all if the government took an even larger role.

These two people represent two basic viewpoints. Some people believe the government should step back. In their opinion, less regulation and fewer taxes would benefit the economy greatly. Others believe that the government does not do enough. In their opinion, more regulation and better goods and services are called for to help strengthen business.

Because the United States is a democracy, the role of the government in the economy can change. Voters may decide to increase or decrease taxes. A government may choose to spend a greater amount on jails than on poverty programs, or vice versa. It may decide whether or not to require stricter air standards. Many of these things depend on the needs of the country, the wishes of voting citizens, and the decisions of elected government leaders.

In a democracy, the people who run the country are elected by the voters.

In the United States, growth in government has been the overall trend since the 1930s. This means more goods and services provided by the government, more regulation, and more taxes. In recent years, however, the government has had to take a serious look at this pattern. You will learn more about this in Chapter 20.

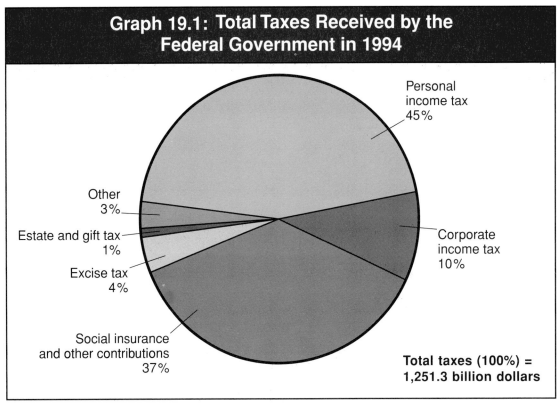

Graph 19.1: Total Taxes Received by the Federal Government in 1994

Personal
income tax
45%

Other
3%

Estate and gift tax
1%

Excise tax
4%

Corporate
income tax
10%

Social insurance
and other contributions
37%

**Total taxes (100%) =
1,251.3 billion dollars**

(Source: Executive Office of the President, Office of Management and Budget. Figures are estimates for 1994, as reported in *1994 Information Please Almanac*)

Economics Practice

Write answers to the following questions on a separate sheet of paper.

1. What are two viewpoints about the role of government in a free market economic system?

2. Look at Graph 19.1. What type of tax provides the greatest amount of dollars to the federal government?

3. What is the second greatest source of tax dollars?

Great Economic Thinkers: Paul Samuelson

Paul Samuelson was the first American to win the Nobel prize in economics. Each year six Nobel prizes are awarded for outstanding work in economics, physics, chemistry, medicine, literature, and world peace.

Samuelson was born in Gary, Indiana, in 1915. After graduating from high school, he studied economics at the University of Chicago and at Harvard.

Samuelson believes the government has an important role to play in the economy. He supports government policies that try to solve the problems of inflation and unemployment. However, he does not believe that there are always simple answers to complicated economic questions.

Samuelson is well known for many things. He has been a professor at MIT for over 30 years. He served as an advisor to President Kennedy in the 1960s. He wrote an economics textbook that has been called the most successful textbook ever published—on any subject. He has written many articles for *Newsweek* magazine.

One of Paul Samuelson's major contributions to economics involves math. While still a student, he wrote papers that described economic ideas in terms of math. This made economics clearer for many people. This is one of the reasons why he was given the Nobel prize in economics.

Paul Anthony Samuelson (1915–   )

Chapter Summary

- Goods and services such as roads, national defense, police protection, and jails are provided by the federal, state, and local governments. The government does this in order to preserve basic rights for all individuals in the U.S. It would be difficult for private businesses to provide these goods and services.

- The government regulates economic activity in the U.S. in the areas of competition, consumer protection, and labor. It also regulates negative effects of economic activity such as pollution.

- Government goods and services are paid for with tax dollars. Certain taxes are paid mainly by those people who will use the goods and services those taxes pay for. This is the case with social insurance programs. Other taxes are paid by everyone who has the ability to pay.

- Some people believe that the government should take a larger role in the free market economy. Others believe that the government should have a very small role. In a democratic nation, the government's role will change with the needs and wishes of voters and elected officials.

Chapter Quiz

Write answers to the following questions on a separate sheet of paper.

A. Thinking About Economics

1. What are the three levels of government that provide goods and services?

2. Give an example of a good or a service provided by each level of government.

3. What might happen if fire protection were left up to private businesses rather than being provided by the government?

4. Explain one way the government tries to ensure that businesses will be able to compete with each other.

5. Give an example of a negative effect of economic activity regulated by the government.

6. What does the Environmental Protection Agency (EPA) do?

7. Why don't most businesses regulate pollution on their own?

8. What is one way the government pays for goods and services?

9. Describe one kind of tax.

10. What are two basic viewpoints about the role of the government in a free market system?

B. Personal Economics

List two types of taxes that you or your family pays. Then list two government goods or services that are paid for with taxes. Do you think these tax dollars are going to good use? Explain.

C. World Economics

The economy of Russia is changing. The government used to control all of the major businesses and industries. Now the government is beginning to play a smaller role in the economy. For the first time in more than 70 years, people are being allowed to own their own businesses. Suppose you lived in Russia, and you wanted to open a restaurant in Moscow. How would owning a restaurant be different from working in a government-owned restaurant?

Chapter 20

The Government Budget and the National Debt

Every year, government leaders must agree on a budget for the United States. The issue is debated in Congress.

Chapter Learning Objectives

- Define the national debt.
- Explain how the government finances the national debt.
- List two facts about the growth of the national debt.

Words to Know

bankrupt   unable to pay debts

budget deficit   a financial situation in which spending is greater than income or revenues

budget surplus   a financial situation in which spending is less than income or revenues

expenditures   expenses

government revenue   tax dollars received by government

national debt   the total amount of money owed by the federal government

Arguing Over the Budget

Joshua and Joan Steinem are married. Every six months, they sit down together and review their income and their bills. Their goal is to plan a budget that will keep them out of debt.

Quite often, Joshua and Joan end up raising their voices during these sessions. Joshua likes to spend money on new things for their home, while Joan believes in saving. After much debate, they usually compromise and agree on a budget.

One night on the news, the couple heard how Congress was arguing about the United States budget. Different groups of representatives had their own ideas about how to spend government money.

"Well," said Joan to Josh, "I guess we're not the only ones with money problems. Even the Congress of the United States argues about going into debt!"

The Government Budget

Like individual households and businesses, all governments have budgets. The money that the government brings in from taxes is **government revenue**. Government leaders then decide how to spend the revenue. They spend money to run the armed forces, for social insurance and social welfare programs, and so forth. These expenses are called **expenditures**.

Suppose that in your own household budget, you spent less than your income. You would have a **budget surplus**. You would have money left over. If you spent more than your income, you would have a **budget deficit**. You would owe someone money. If you have a balanced budget, you would not spend more than you took in.

The same principles are at work in governments. In the federal government, for example, there was a budget surplus in 1960. The government took in 269 million more dollars in revenue than it spent. In 1970, the government spent about 123 billion dollars more than it took in. This created a budget deficit.

The federal government has not had a balanced budget since 1800. And it has not had a budget surplus since 1969.

Borrowing and the National Debt

How can the government spend more than it has? In Chapter 7, you read about government bonds. When the government cannot cover its expenditures with tax revenues, it borrows money by selling bonds. You may remember that a bond is an I.O.U. People who buy government bonds are lending the government money. With many bonds, the government pays interest until the bond matures. Then the government repays the original amount loaned.

The **national debt** is the federal government's total amount of outstanding debt. It is all the money that the federal government owes. Graph 20.1 shows just how much the national debt has increased over the last 30 years. In 1960, the government owed about 289 billion dollars. In 1992, the national debt had reached over 4 trillion dollars. This 4 trillion dollars was not just the deficit for 1992. It also takes into account all the deficits from prior years. The annual interest paid to borrowers on this amount was about 2 billion dollars. Over 20 percent of the total federal budget went toward paying this interest.

Graph 20.1: National Debt

(Source: Bureau of Public Debt, U.S. Department of the Treasury as reported in the *1994 World Almanac and Book of Facts*)

Economics Practice

Write your answers to the following questions on a separate sheet of paper.

1. If the government spends more money than it takes in, is there a budget deficit or surplus?

2. If the government spends less money than it takes in, is there a budget deficit or surplus?

3. What is the national debt?

The National Debt Debate

In recent years, some government leaders have called for an end to the growth in the national debt. Why? One concern is their worry that government spending is replacing private spending in the economy. Suppose the government borrows more and more money to cover its spending. That leaves less money available for private citizens and private businesses to borrow. Government leaders also worry about the growing amount of interest on the debt. They are concerned that the debt will eventually mean higher taxes for U.S. citizens.

Although the national debt has grown very large in recent years, it does not mean the government is going **bankrupt**. Unlike a business, it can always raise revenue through taxes. If it wanted to pay back the debt, it could do so by raising taxes. Some of the tax dollars that Americans pay go toward paying the interest on the debt. But for the most part, other Americans receive those interest payments. So nothing real is lost for the economy as a whole. There could be a problem, however, if a large amount of interest is paid to foreign investors. This would mean that American tax dollars leave the country to pay the interest. This would be a drain on the United States' economy. It could cause a problem for future generations of Americans who pay the interest on the money that is borrowed today. How much would every person in America have to pay in taxes to pay off the national debt? The per capita debt gives you this information. The table on page 261 shows how this debt has changed since 1800.

Per Capita Public Debt	
Year	Amount
1800	$15.87
1860	$2.06
1900	$16.60
1930	$131.51
1945	$1,845.60
1960	$1,572.31
1970	$1,807.09
1980	$2,969.55
1990	$12,823.28
1992	$15,650.00

(Source: Department of the Treasury, Financial Management Services as reported in *1994 Information Please Almanac*)

Per capita means each person

Economics Practice

Write answers to the following questions on a separate sheet of paper.

1. Why would some government leaders like to see the national debt stop growing?

2. Some people argue that the national debt will not cause the federal government to go bankrupt. Why?

3. Look at the table above. How much would each person in the U.S. have paid to meet the national debt in 1990?

Great Economic Thinkers: John Maynard Keynes

**John Maynard Keynes
(1883–1946)**

John Maynard Keynes was a British economist who lived from 1883 to 1946. His ideas about the Great Depression in the 1930s changed the way that many people think about government spending.

During the Great Depression, millions of people were unemployed in Europe and the United States. Many people said that the government didn't need to get involved to help end depressions or recessions. But Keynes disagreed with them.

In 1936 Keynes wrote a book called *The General Theory of Employment, Interest and Money.* In this book he described a way to end depressions. He said the government should spend money on programs which would give people jobs. Keynes wrote that this would be a good idea even if the government went into debt.

Keynes was famous before *The General Theory* was published. He had already written other important books. He was very rich from buying and selling stocks and foreign currencies. He was married to a beautiful Russian ballerina.

Chapter Review

Chapter Summary

- All governments have budgets. The government takes in revenue through taxes and spends it on various programs, goods, and services. When a government takes in more than it spends, there is a surplus. When it spends more than it takes in, there is a deficit.

- To pay for deficits, the government borrows money through the sale of bonds. The government then pays interest on the borrowed money. The total of all money owed by the federal government is called the national debt.

- The national debt has been growing steadily over the last thirty years. Some people are alarmed by the 4 trillion dollar debt. They say it could cause a big increase in taxes. Others say the government can always pay off the debt by raising taxes. It is doubtful that the government would ever need to do this. Unlike a business, it can finance the debt and interest by borrowing more money as long as people want to buy government bonds.

Chapter Quiz

Write answers to the following questions on a separate sheet of paper.

A. Thinking About Economics

1. What are revenues?

2. What are expenditures?

3. When is there a budget surplus?

4. When is there a budget deficit?

5. What does it mean to have a balanced budget?

6. Suppose the government wants to spend more than it has in revenues. How does it get the money?

7. What is the national debt?

8. A large portion of the federal budget goes toward interest payments. Who gets these payments, and why?

9. Give one reason why some government leaders want to halt the growth of the national debt.

10. Some government leaders argue that the government will not go bankrupt. What is their reasoning?

B. Personal Economics

Suppose there is a budget deficit in your own state government. State lawmakers must balance the budget. They can either raise taxes or cut spending in all state government programs. Which would you favor? Why?

C. World Economics

Graph 20.3 shows how the U.S. national debt as a percentage of national output compares to that of other leading industrial countries. These are the estimated figures for 1988. Use the graph to answer the following questions.

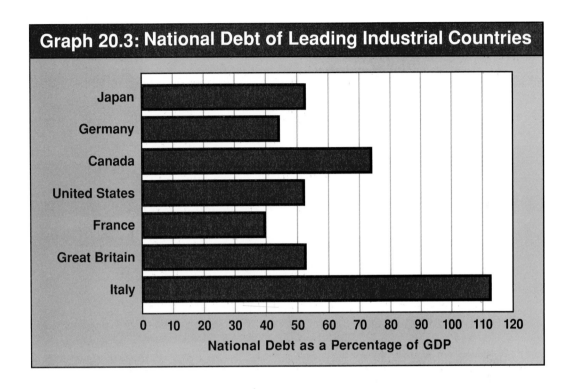

Graph 20.3: National Debt of Leading Industrial Countries

National Debt as a Percentage of GDP

a. In which countries is the national debt as a percentage of national output greater than in the United States?

b. In which countries is the national debt less than in the United States?

c. In which country is the national debt greater than the national output?

d. The national debt in the United States is what percentage of the U.S. national output?

Chapter 21

Trying to Solve the Economy's Problems

The government created thousands of jobs to reduce unemployment during the Great Depression. In this WPA work program in 1935, curb stones were removed in order to make the street wider.

Chapter Learning Objectives

- Explain how fiscal policy is used to control inflation and unemployment.
- Explain how monetary policy is used to control inflation and unemployment.
- Describe three ways the Federal Reserve can affect the money supply.
- Explain the supply-side theory of economics.

Words to Know

discount rate   the rate of interest charged by the Federal Reserve Bank to borrowing banks

fiscal policy   the government program of increasing or decreasing taxes and government spending to control inflation and unemployment

monetary policy   the Federal Reserve Bank program of increasing or decreasing the money supply to control inflation and unemployment

prime rate   the lowest rate of interest that banks offer their best business customers

reserve requirement   the amount of money a bank must keep in its vault or on deposit at the Fed to back up its customer's deposits.

supply-side economics   the belief that high unemployment and inflation can be solved by encouraging people and businesses to produce more

The Effects of Economic Ideas

Theresa Anguin wants to buy a house, but she discovers that the interest rates are high. This would make her house payments so high that she wouldn't be able to buy the house. The bank tells her the interest rates will remain high for a while. Theresa must wait for them to go down so she can afford the house.

Niles Hathaway is looking for a job. He has been unemployed for a long time. He hears that the government may start a job program in his city. This gives him some hope.

Heidi Lawton is a store owner. A new tax law favoring business now saves her money. She decides to open a second store. She will hire eight new workers to help her.

All these people have something in common. They have been affected by economic policies that are used to try to help the economy. The government and the Federal Reserve try to control inflation and unemployment. They try to do things to help the economy grow. This chapter looks at some of these policies and how they can affect you.

Fiscal Policy

Fiscal policy means that the government increases or decreases taxes and spending to control inflation and unemployment. Here is an example of how fiscal policy might be used to control unemployment. Suppose that the unemployment rate is very high, around nine percent. Consumer spending is down because so many people are jobless. This means that businesses produce fewer goods and services.

The government must find ways to create jobs. One way to do this might be to increase government spending. For example, the government might decide to spend money to build new roads. It hires unemployed workers to build the roads. These workers now have wages to spend on consumer goods. In this way, consumer demand will be increased by government spending. Businesses will expand. More jobs are created.

With fiscal policy, high unemployment calls for higher government spending and lower taxes.

The government might also decrease taxes to increase spending. This also leads to more jobs. Suppose the government cuts everyone's taxes. Consumers would have more income to spend on consumer goods and services. As consumers spend more, businesses produce more. And more people get jobs.

When using fiscal policy, the government will do just the *opposite* to control inflation. Remember that inflation means that prices are going up. This happens when consumer demand is high. When businesses cannot meet this high demand, prices go up. Too many dollars are chasing too few goods and services. So the government tries to limit spending to keep prices from going up.

To do this, it may decrease government spending or raise taxes. Both will cause people to have less money to spend on consumer goods. If the government decides to stop building new roads, some workers will lose their jobs. They'll have less money to spend. If taxes go up, people have to pay more to the government. They will then have less money to spend on themselves. As consumer demand decreases, businesses will be less likely to raise prices.

With fiscal policy, high inflation calls for less government spending and higher taxes.

Some economists do not think fiscal policy works. They say that it takes too long for changes in taxes or government spending to be put into effect. Then, when the changes do occur, there is no strong evidence that they work. For example, government spending was increased during the 1930s to help America out of the Great Depression. The government created thousands of job programs to boost consumer spending and to try to eliminate unemployment. However, unemployment remained high throughout the decade until the beginning of World War II.

Presidents Franklin D. Roosevelt, John F. Kennedy, and Lyndon B. Johnson all believed in strong fiscal policy.

Economics Practice

Write answers to the following questions on a separate sheet of paper.

1. Suppose that there is high unemployment. The government wants to use fiscal policy to try to create jobs. What two things might the government do?

2. What two things might the same government do to slow down inflation?

3. Why do some economists think fiscal policy does not work very well?

Monetary Policy

Many economists believe that controlling the money supply is the key to controlling inflation and unemployment. They believe in using monetary policy. **Monetary policy** means that the Federal Reserve Bank takes action to control inflation and unemployment. It does this by increasing or decreasing the money supply.

Suppose there is high unemployment. If the Federal Reserve takes action to increase the money supply, then consumers and businesses have more money to spend. This will lead to more goods and services being produced, and more jobs.

Now, suppose there is high inflation. The Federal Reserve will want to decrease the money supply. Fewer dollars in the economy mean that consumers will spend less. And as consumer demand slows down, so will rising prices.

Economics Practice

Answer the following questions on a separate sheet of paper.

1. What is meant by monetary policy?

2. Why does more money in the economy help to reduce unemployment?

3. Why does less money in the economy help to reduce inflation?

How the Federal Reserve Controls the Money Supply

How does the Federal Reserve control the money supply? As you may recall from Chapter 14, the Federal Reserve regulates banks in the United States. To increase the money supply, the Federal Reserve encourages banks to make loans. When banks lend money, consumers and businesses have more money to spend. This increases the money supply. To decrease the money supply, the Federal Reserve discourages bank loans. The Federal Reserve encourages or discourages bank loans by taking action in three ways:

1. *Changing reserve requirements.* You learned in Chapter 14 what happens when someone deposits $100 cash into a bank. The bank doesn't keep all of the $100 to back up that deposit. It might keep $15, for example, and loan out the rest. The bank must keep a certain amount on hand in its vault or on deposit at the Federal Reserve Bank. This is called the **reserve requirement.** The Federal Reserve Board sets the reserve requirements for banks.

   When the reserve requirements are lowered, banks have more money to loan. This helps to increase the money supply. When reserve requirements are raised, banks have less money to loan. This helps to decrease the money supply.

2. *Changing the discount rate.* Sometimes, banks cannot meet their reserve requirements. This may happen if customers withdraw large amounts of money, a loan does not get repaid, and so forth. Sometimes, banks simply want more reserves so they can loan more money. In these cases, the bank may choose to borrow money from the Federal Reserve Bank. The rate of interest charged by the Federal Reserve Bank is called the **discount rate.**

   Often, you know what the Federal Reserve is doing with the money supply when you hear news about the discount rate. Suppose the Federal Reserve has a low discount rate. Banks will be more likely to borrow from the Federal Reserve. Because these banks borrowed at a low rate, they can usually offer lower interest rates to their customers. The **prime rate** is the lowest rate of interest that banks offer their best business customers. Customers will be attracted by these low interest rates. As more loans are made and more interest is paid, the money supply will increase.

If the discount rate is high, banks will be less likely to borrow from the Fed. When they do borrow or make loans, they will charge higher interest rates on the customer loans. This will discourage consumers and businesses from taking out loans. The money supply will decrease.

3. *Buying and selling securities.* The Federal Reserve Bank can buy and sell government bonds just like you can. Suppose that the Fed wants to increase the money supply. It buys bonds and pays money to the seller. The seller than puts this money into the bank. Part of it is loaned out and the money supply increases.

To decrease the money supply, the Federal Reserve Bank will do just the opposite. It will sell bonds. The money it gets will be taken out of circulation. The money supply will decrease.

The Federal Open Market Committee (FOMC) makes decisions about the buying and selling of government bonds. The sale and purchase of government bonds by the Fed is known as open-market operations.

Securities generally means stocks and bonds. In this case the Fed is buying and selling U.S. government bonds.

Economics Practice

Answer the following questions on a separate sheet of paper.

1. Suppose inflation is high. The Federal Reserve takes action to decrease the money supply by increasing the discount rate. How will this probably affect bank loans to customers like you?

2. Suppose that unemployment is high. The Federal Reserve Bank takes action to increase the money supply by decreasing its discount rate. How will this probably affect bank loans to customers like you?

Supply-Side Economic Theory

During the 1980s, a different type of economic policy was tried in the United States. It was called **supply-side economics.** Supply-side economists have their own ideas for dealing with high unemployment and inflation. They believe the problem can be solved by increasing the amount of goods and services (supply) produced in the economy. They believe that the way to do this is to cut taxes and decrease the size of government. They believe that people would work harder if they got to keep more of their money. The harder they worked, the more they would spend and invest. Private businesses would respond to this spending by producing more. Thus unemployment would be lowered as well as inflation. Using these supply-side ideas, the federal government greatly reduced income taxes for many Americans in the 1980s.

President Ronald Reagan strongly believed in supply-side economic ideas. He acted on his beliefs by cutting taxes during his administration in the 1980s.

Great Economic Thinkers: Milton Friedman

Some economists believe that fiscal policy and monetary policy do not work very well. They think that these policies may cause, rather than cure, the economy's problems. Milton Friedman is one of these economists.

Milton Friedman was born in New York in 1912. His parents were poor immigrants. He earned a scholarship to college, and studied economics in New Jersey, New York, and Chicago. He was a professor at the University of Chicago for many years, and was awarded the Nobel prize in Economics in 1976. Since 1977, he has worked at the Hoover Institution in California.

Milton Friedman believes that the amount of money in the economy is very important. However, he doesn't think the Federal Reserve should keep

(Milton Friedman (1912–   )

changing the money supply to try to cure inflation or unemployment. He thinks the Fed should follow set rules for the money supply. For example, the Fed should try to have the money supply grow at the same rate that GDP is growing.

Friedman says that when government gets larger, people have less personal freedom. When the government uses fiscal policy to tax and spend, the government is spending instead of the people. Friedman believes that fiscal policy results in taking spending decisions away from the people.

Milton Friedman also thinks that we should have a pure free market economy. Then the problems of inflation and unemployment could cure themselves. He does not think that the government and the Fed know enough to be able to "fine-tune" the economy. By using fiscal and monetary policies, they end up making things worse.

Chapter Review

Chapter Summary

- When using fiscal policy, the government increases or decreases government spending and taxes to control unemployment and inflation. If there is high unemployment, the government increases spending and lowers taxes. This encourages consumer spending and thus production of goods and services. If inflation is high, the government decreases spending and raises taxes. This discourages consumer spending and causes businesses to limit price increases.

- Under monetary policy, the Federal Reserve Bank increases or decreases the money supply to control unemployment and inflation. When unemployment is high, the Fed tries to increase the money supply. This encourages spending and businesses expand. When inflation is high, the Fed tries to decrease the money supply. This limits spending and causes businesses to limit price increases.

- The Federal Reserve Bank controls the money supply by encouraging or discouraging bank loans. The Fed does this by changing the reserve requirements, changing the discount rate, and by buying or selling government bonds.

- Supply-side economic ideas call for lower taxes and a decrease in the size of government. This should encourage people to supply more goods and services. The belief is that people will work harder if they get to keep more of their income. Thus, consumer spending will go up and businesses will expand. This will help limit both inflation and unemployment.

Chapter Quiz

Write answers to the following questions on a separate sheet of paper.

A. Thinking About Economics

1. What is fiscal policy?

2. How would the government use fiscal policy during times of unemployment?

3. How would the government use fiscal policy during times of inflation?

4. What is monetary policy?

5. Using monetary policy, what would the Federal Reserve Bank try to do to the money supply during times of unemployment? Why?

6. Using monetary policy what would the Federal Reserve Bank try to do to the money supply during times of inflation? Why?

7. To decrease the money supply and limit bank loans, what might the Federal Reserve Bank do to reserve requirements?

8. To increase the money supply and limit bank loans, what might the Federal Reserve Bank do to the discount rate?

9. How do supply-side economists believe that unemployment and inflation can be solved?

10. How do supply-side economists believe that supply can be increased?

B. Personal Economics

Suppose you hear on the news that the discount rate is going down. What do you think the Federal Reserve is trying to do? Is this a good time or bad time for you to get a loan? Explain.

C. World Economics

Recently Argentina has been suffering from high inflation. The yearly inflation rate in March 1991 was 132 percent. But in April, it had fallen to 66 percent. The government had come up with a plan to fight inflation. It decided to go after corporations and individuals who had not been paying their taxes. Also, the government began to put pressure on various companies in certain key industries to lower their prices. Those who lowered their prices became eligible to get loans at special low rates. If the government of Argentina used fiscal policy to control inflation, what would they have done? Explain your answer.

Unit Seven Review

Write answers to the following questions on a separate sheet of paper.

1. What are two examples of goods or services provided by the government?

2. What is one way that the government raises money?

3. Why does the government take a role in regulating things such as pollution?

4. What is the difference between a budget surplus and a budget deficit?

5. How does the government raise the money to pay for a budget deficit?

6. What is the national debt?

7. Suppose there is high unemployment. To solve this problem, the government uses fiscal policy: it spends more and lowers taxes. Why does taking these steps help cure unemployment?

8. Suppose there is high inflation. Using fiscal policy, what might the government do to try to cure the inflation?

9. Using monetary policy, should the government decrease or increase the money supply during times of inflation? Why?

10. What is the discount rate?

A Global View

Chapter 22
International Trade

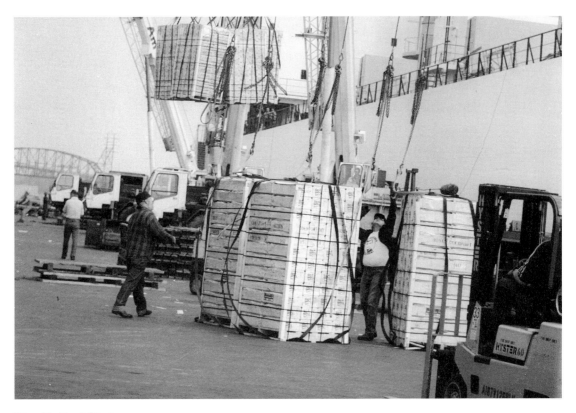

The United States trades with countries all around the world. Trade has increased partly because of improved transportation.

Chapter Learning Objectives
- Explain how specialization and trade are related.
- List two benefits of international trade.
- List two ways that a country can limit trade.

Words to Know

comparative advantage   a country's ability to produce a product at a lower opportunity cost than other countries

embargo   a government policy that cuts off trade with certain countries

exports   goods sold to other countries

free trade   unrestricted trade between countries

import quota   a law that sets a fixed amount of imports

imports   goods bought from other countries

international trade   trade between nations

protectionism   the policy of limiting trade with other countries to protect domestic industries

protective tariff   a tax meant to raise the price of an imported good in order to protect a certain industry from foreign competition

revenue tariff   an import tax used to provide government revenue

tariff   a tax on imports

trade deficit   a condition in which the value of a nation's imports is greater than the value of its exports

trade surplus   a condition in which the value of a nation's exports is greater than the value of its imports

Paul Sanchez lives in California. On a typical day, he eats bananas from Guatemala in his cereal. He gets into a car that was made in Japan and drives to school. Sometimes he stops for gasoline that was refined from Middle Eastern oil.

Paul's father works in a computer manufacturing company. In recent years, the demand for these computers has gone up in other countries. The computers are used in schools and businesses around the world.

Though Paul may not think about it, he buys **imports**, goods bought from other countries. His father makes **exports**, goods that will be sold to other countries. **International trade**, or trade between countries, is an important part of many countries' economies.

Trade and Specialization

International trade has been going on since ancient times. As people began to travel, they found that countries differed widely in the amount and quality of their productive resources. One country might have fertile land, another acres of forest. And still another might have resources such as iron and copper.

How the people in a country used these resources varied, too. For example, early cultures in ancient China produced silk. Meanwhile, Ceylon produced pearls and spices, India produced cotton and precious stones, and Arabia produced cinnamon and incense. Merchants from these countries began trading with each other. They established trade routes leading from one country to another. Countries and cultures specialized in different goods and services, depending on their resources and costs. Trade between countries enabled people to share in these different specialties.

In today's world, trade is easier and more extensive, partly due to improved transportation. Imports and exports move tens of thousands of miles in a few days' time, if need be. Countries become known for certain products. For example, Japan is well known for its electronics exports. The United States is recognized as a major exporter of wheat. Fine African coffee is bought throughout the world.

Do you own or use a product imported from another country?

How do countries come to specialize in certain exports? They specialize in making products where they have the comparative advantage. **Comparative advantage** means that a country can produce a product at a lower opportunity cost than other countries. For example, the United States imports baskets. The United States certainly has the resources necessary to produce more than enough baskets to meet its demand. But baskets can be produced much more cheaply in certain other countries. These countries have the comparative advantage when it comes to producing baskets. So the United States doesn't bother to specialize in baskets. Instead, it imports baskets from those countries that *do* specialize in baskets. And the United States uses its own resources for producing other goods.

Silk made with the help of these silkworms has long been an export of China.

Economics Practice

Write answers to the following questions on a separate sheet of paper.

1. What are exports? Give an example of a good exported by the United States.

2. What are imports? Give an example of a good imported by the United States.

3. What is meant by comparative advantage?

The Benefits and Problems of International Trade

International trade allows countries to specialize and use their resources in the best way possible. This means that world production is increased. It also means that people get to consume more and better products, at lower prices, than if there were no trade.

But some people believe that international trade can also cause problems. For example, countries may become dependent on the goods of another country. The United States imports a great deal of foreign oil, for example. Middle Eastern countries can produce oil at lower costs than the United States can.

When one nation trades with another, both countries are importing and exporting certain products. The value of a nation's imports and exports may not be equal. When the dollar value of exports is greater than the dollar value of imports, the nation is said to have a **trade surplus**. When the value of imports is greater than the value of exports, there is a **trade deficit**.

In recent years, the United States has built up a large trade deficit with some of its trading partners. In 1985, for example, Japanese companies exported about $50 billion more in goods to the United States than American firms exported to Japan. Other countries, such as Korea, Taiwan, Singapore, and Hong Kong, have flooded American markets with low-cost imports. American consumers bought the imports instead of American products because the imports were cheaper. Another major cause of the growing trade deficit was the rise in the cost of imported oil. The price of a barrel of oil went from less than $2 in the early 1970s to $35 in the early 1980s. And in 1980, foreign oil amounted to about 40 percent of American imports.

Many people believe that a large trade deficit points to problems in a nation's economy. The U.S. trade deficit may indicate a loss of American jobs and lessened ability to compete with foreign producers.

Since the mid–1970's the United States has had large trade deficits.

Economics Practice

Write answers to the following questions on a separate sheet of paper.

1. What are two benefits of international trade?

2. Give one example of a country becoming dependent on another country for a particular product.

3. What is a trade deficit? Why might it be a problem?

Limiting Trade: Free Trade vs. Protectionism

Many of the clothes you buy are made in other countries. You bought imported clothing because you liked the style and you thought the price was fair. When Americans buy imported goods, American companies lose business. They may have to close plants and lay off workers. Some people argue that competition from foreign countries is healthy in a market economy. Consumers benefit by being able to buy the imports. It forces American businesses to produce better-quality goods at fair prices. People who favor this competition believe in **free trade**. With free trade, countries have no or few restrictions on imports and exports.

People who believe trade should be limited by tariffs and quotas favor **protectionism.**

In 1990, there was an import quota on women's and girls' cotton shirts from Taiwan. Only 326,625 could be imported into the U.S.

Almost all countries use tariffs and quotas. A **tariff** is a tax on imports. There are two kinds of tariffs. **Revenue tariffs** are taxes meant to bring in government revenue. Some products also have a **protective tariff**. This type of tariff is meant to raise the price of an imported good in order to protect a certain industry. For example, clothing is imported into the United States from many countries. Other countries produce clothing at lower costs than the United States does. As a result, the imported goods cost much less than the same type of good made in the United States. This is a benefit for U.S. consumers. But people who work in the U.S. clothing industry would like to keep their jobs. To protect the clothing industry, the United States might impose a protective tariff on imported clothing. Consumers might be more likely to "buy American" if the imported goods were more expensive.

Another way to limit the number of imports is to use **import quotas**. An import quota restricts the quantity of a certain item imported into a country. For example, a country might allow only 50,000 German-made cars to be imported each year. Like protective tariffs, quotas are meant to protect certain industries from foreign competition. In 1981, the United States was planning to set a quota on the number of Japanese cars allowed into the country. To prevent this, Japan agreed to place voluntary restrictions on the number of cars exported to the United States. The Japanese agreed to a limit of 1.7 million cars a year. In 1985 the limit was raised to 2.3 million cars a year.

Sometimes a nation or group of nations will call for an **embargo**. This means that they will try to prevent trade with a certain country or countries. This situation usually arises only during times of war or other serious political crisis. For example, in 1973 a war broke out between Israel and its Arab neighbors.

The Arabs were angry at the United States because of U.S. support for Israel. So they called for an oil embargo to punish the United States and its friends. As a result, the price of gasoline in the United States skyrocketed.

In 1980 President Jimmy Carter placed an embargo on U.S. grain sales to the Soviet Union. He did this in response to the Soviet invasion of Afghanistan in 1979. Sometimes a nation will place a total embargo on all trade with a particular country to protest a political situation. The United States placed such an embargo on Cuba in 1961 and on Nicaragua in 1985. South Africa has had a partial trade embargo, or economic sanctions, placed on it because of its racist policies. And in 1990 Iraq was punished with an almost total trade embargo because of its invasion of Kuwait.

On January 1, 1994, the North American Free Trade Agreement (NAFTA) went into effect. NAFTA allows the U.S., Mexico, and Canada to gradually stop tariffs over the next 15 years. Since the U.S. already had a free trade agreement with Canada, the results of NAFTA will be with Mexico.

It has been estimated that a U.S. family of four pays over $400 per year in tariffs and quotas on clothing and textiles. With GATT this should decrease.

People who support NAFTA feel it will help the U.S. It will be easier for U.S. companies to export goods to Mexico. This will create more jobs for people in the U.S. The auto and computer industries will benefit most.

Economics Practice

Write answers to the following questions on a separate sheet of paper.

1. What does NAFTA mean?

2. Who might benefit from NAFTA and GATT?
   Explain your answer.

People against NAFTA feel it will result in a loss of U.S. jobs. NAFTA will make it easier for U.S. companies to build factories in Mexico. Most Mexican workers earn less than U.S. workers. Some U.S. companies may decide to hire only Mexican workers.

Most economists believe NAFTA will help people. U.S. consumers will not have to spend as much money for Mexican goods. Many people in the U.S. will get jobs selling goods to Mexico.

GATT (General Agreement on Tariffs and Trade) is another important free trade agreement. On December 15, 1993, 115 nations agreed to decrease tariffs worldwide. GATT, like NAFTA, encourages free trade.

U.S. consumers should benefit from GATT because of lower prices. U.S. producers should benefit because it will be easier to sell their goods to other countries.

Some U.S. companies were disappointed with GATT. For example, moviemakers were unhappy. France still has quotas for the number of American television programs that can be aired. Tariffs are still added to ticket prices for American movies shown in France. This means moviemakers cannot sell as much as they would like in France.

NAFTA and GATT are important steps toward free world trade. Free trade allows countries to benefit from specialization and helps people.

What It Means to Me: Exchange Rates

As you know, different countries use different types of money or currency. For example, the United States uses the dollar, the French use the franc, and the Japanese use the yen. If you ever travel to a foreign country, you will learn to exchange your American dollars for different types of currency. Usually, this exchange is done at a bank.

How do you know how much your American dollar is worth? It depends on the *exchange rate*. This is the rate set by supply and demand for different kinds of currency in various countries. Exchange rates change often. For example, one day a dollar may buy 138 yen and the next day only 137.

If you are interested in learning what your dollar is worth on the international market, look in the travel section of your local newspaper. You will find a chart that looks something like this:

Country/Currency	$1 U.S. Equals	Foreign Currency in U.S. $
Austria/schilling	11.89	0.08
Denmark/krone	6.47	0.15
Thailand/baht	25.35	0.04

The chart shows you what the U.S. dollar is worth on that day. For example, your one U.S. dollar will get you almost 12 Austrian schillings. If an Austrian came to the United States, he or she would get about 8 cents for each schilling.

Can you tell what $1 was worth in Denmark and Thailand on the day this chart was made?

Chapter Review

Chapter Summary

- Most countries in the world participate in international trade. They import certain goods and export others. By doing so, countries can specialize, world production is increased, and people can consume more and better-quality goods and services.

- Countries specialize because they have a comparative advantage over other countries. This means that they can produce a good at a lower opportunity cost than other countries. Through specialization and exchange, countries become better off.

- In the short run, international trade may cause a country to become dependent on other countries for certain goods.

- In some cases, competition from imports can hurt certain industries. To restrict this competition, countries sometimes use protective tariffs and quotas.

- A trade deficit is a condition in which the value of a nation's imports is greater than the value of its exports. A trade surplus is a condition in which the value of a nation's exports is greater than the value of its imports.

- In 1993-94, two major free trade agreements, NAFTA and GATT, took place. Both promise to reduce tariffs on many imports. Consumers should benefit from lower prices. Producers should benefit because it will be easier to sell exports.

Chapter Quiz

Write answers to the following questions on a separate sheet of paper.

A. Thinking About Economics

1. What is an import?

2. What is an export?

3. How does international trade help increase world production?

4. What is meant by comparative advantage?

5. Give an example of international trade causing a country to become dependent on another country for a product.

6. What is meant by a trade deficit?

7. What is meant by a trade surplus?

8. How do tariffs affect the price of imports?

9. What is the purpose of tariffs and quotas?

10. How can consumers benefit from NAFTA and GATT?

B. Personal Economics

What if you worked in the U.S. auto industry. Would you be for or against high tariffs on Japanese cars? How would you feel if you were a consumer who was buying an imported car? Explain.

C. World Economics

Has the U.S. become too dependent on foreign oil? Did this dependence help create U.S. involvement in Operation Desert Storm?

Chapter 23
Developing Countries

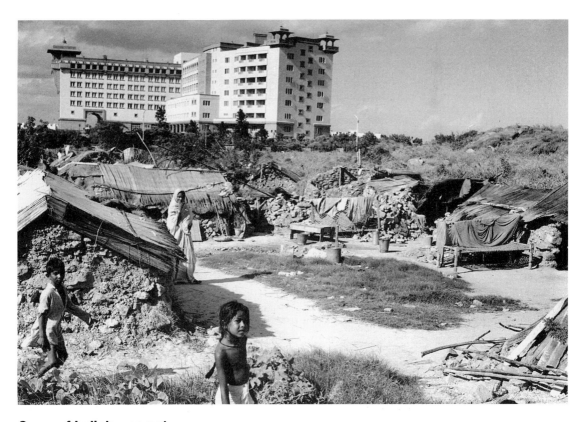

Some of India's poorest people live in these mud brick huts in New Delhi. Yet right next door is the Ashoka, one of Asia's finest luxury hotels. Such an extreme contrast between poverty and wealth is common in many developing nations.

Chapter Learning Objectives

- Compare and contrast developed and developing countries.
- Explain two ways in which developed countries try to aid developing countries.
- Describe two common problems in developing nations and list some possible solutions.

Words to Know

developed countries   countries that are highly industrialized and have a higher standard of living than developing countries

developing countries   countries that depend mainly on agriculture instead of industry and have a lower standard of living than developed countries

foreign aid   aid that one country gives to another in the form of money, capital resources, and food

infant mortality rate   the percentage of infants who die during their first year

life expectancy   the number of years that an average person can expect to live

literacy rate   the percentage of people in a population who can read and write

per capita GDP   GDP of a country divided by the number of people in the population; a measure of a country's wealth compared to other countries

subsistence farming   farming that produces enough food for the farming family to live on, but nothing more

---

The scene is the city of Bombay in India. Below the modern high-rise buildings, a movie company is shooting a film. In the crowded streets, business people rush to and from work, dressed in their finest suits.

This could be a description of a typical large American city. But the similarity ends here. Just beyond the modern part of Bombay is a completely different scene. Standing almost in the shadows of the high-rises are rough shacks made of cloth and scrap iron. The land for many miles around is covered by this city of shacks.

Among the many thousands of poor people who live here is a young Indian boy named Thiagi. He and his family have left their small farming village to seek a better life. In the village, Thiagi and his sisters had no opportunity to go to school. And the family made very little money farming. They have brought with them very few belongings: their clothing, a few tools, a supply of rice and vegetables. So far, they can find no work and food is scarce. Yet, looking at the lights of the city, they can't help but believe that a better life awaits them.

The story of Thiagi and his family is a common one in developing countries of the world. What are developing countries? What part do other countries play in their development?

Developed vs. Developing Countries

Go into any American city. What do you see? Skyscrapers loom over subways, buses, and cars. People rush to and from jobs in offices and factories. Store shelves are stocked with goods ranging from canned beans to eye make-up. Planes fly overhead, while radios and TVs blare the latest music and news.

Now travel to smaller American villages and towns. Life may be a little quieter and slower. But you will almost always find modern comforts such as hot running water and electricity. Even an isolated Iowa farmer, miles from any city, has the latest farming equipment. In school, his children use computers as they learn to read.

The United States is one of the world's developed countries. **Developed countries** have highly industrialized economies. The use of modern machinery and methods of production is widespread. The populations in developed countries often have good schools and health care available to them. Even the very poor in these countries have a high standard of living, compared to other parts of the world. Japan, Canada, and many of the European nations are some other developed nations.

Life is quite different for the three-quarters of the world's population who live in developing countries. There is very little industry in **developing countries**. Some developing countries, such as India, may have large, modern cities. But large portions of the population barely have enough food to eat. When compared to developed countries, the standard of living in developing countries is quite low.

Developing countries are also called *less developed countries*, or *LDCs*.

Economics Practice

Write answers to the following questions on a separate sheet of paper.

1. How does the amount of industry in developed countries compare to that of developing countries?

2. How does the standard of living in developed countries compare to that of developing countries?

Characteristics of Developing Countries

In previous chapters, you read about the different ways that economic health is measured in the United States. For example, economists and government leaders may look at GDP, inflation, unemployment rates, and the number of people in poverty. Likewise, economists and world leaders look at several different things to determine whether a country is a developing nation.

Of the 168 countries in the world, only about 30 are considered developed.

Remember that GDP is the total dollar value of the final goods and services produced in a country each year.

1. *Developing countries usually have a low per capita GDP.* If you take a country's GDP and divide it by the number of people in the population, you get the **per capita GDP**. Per capita GDP is a way to compare the wealth and productivity of countries and their people.

    In developing countries, per capita GDP is usually below $2,000. For example, Vietnam's per capita GDP is about $200 per year. Compare this to the United States' per capita GDP of almost $20,000. The average person in Vietnam not only has less to spend. He or she has fewer goods and services to spend it on.

Bhutan is the poorest of the LDCs. Per capita GDP in Bhutan is only about $80 per year.

2. *Developing countries usually have agricultural economies.* In a developing country, most people make a living by farming rather than industry. Quite often, a large portion of the population lives through **subsistence farming**. This means that a family produces only enough food for its own needs. In the country of Chile, for example, about 85 percent of the labor force works in farming. Most of these farmers grow only enough food for their own families. In the United States, only about 2 percent of the labor force works in farming. Yet U.S. farmers produce most of the country's food and enough to export, too.

3. *Developing countries have a low literacy rate.* The **literacy rate** is the percentage of people who can read and write. In developing countries, there may not be much money spent for public schools and education. Literacy rates vary greatly among developing nations. In the developing nation of Mozambique, for instance, the literacy rate is 14 percent. This means that out of every 100 people, only 14 can read and write. But in Thailand, another developing nation, the literacy rate is 89 percent. This is close to the U.S. literacy rate of about 99 percent.

4. *Developing countries have poor health conditions.*
Some countries do not have money to develop industries or schools. That usually means they don't have money or know-how for good health care, either. There are few hospitals and doctors, and they are hard to get to. Because of poor health care, people may not live as long as they do in developed nations. Their **life expectancy** is low. For example, the average American male can expect to live to around 72 years of age. But in Peru, a developing country, the life expectancy for the average male is only around 61.

   Also in developing countries, more babies may die during their first year than in developed nations. The number of these deaths per 1,000 babies is called the **infant mortality rate**. In the United States, the infant mortality rate is about 1 percent. This means that about 10 in every 1,000 infants that are born die before the age of 1. In the developing country of Afghanistan, about 19 percent of infants die before the age of 1.

5. *Developing countries have fast-growing populations.*
When a country has trouble feeding its people, a fast-growing population adds to the problem. In many developing nations, the population rate is increasing at over 3 percent each year. This may not seem like much. But in a country such as Honduras, it means the population will double in about 20 years. In the United States, the population is growing at a rate of about 1 percent.

   In 1993, India was the world's second most populous country, with almost 900 million people. China was first with over one billion. Both India and China have population growth rates of about 2.1 percent. They will probably continue to have the world's largest populations into the 21st century.

In 1989, the United Nations made a list of the world's poorest LDCs. It included Afghanistan, Bangladesh, Chad, Haiti, Nepal, Sierra Leone, and Uganda, to name a few.

Economics Practice

Write answers to the following questions on a separate sheet of paper.

1. What is meant by per capita GDP?

2. The per capita GDP of Zaire is about $180. Would you guess that Zaire is a developed or developing country? Why?

3. What are four factors other than per capita GDP that help determine whether a country is developed or developing?

The Challenge of Developing Nations

Developed nations such as the United States often have a great interest in helping developing nations. Helping these countries industrialize can mean more business for the United States. In addition, many people feel a *moral responsibility* toward the citizens in developing countries. They believe good health care and education are basic human rights that everyone in the world should have.

Businesses and banks in developed countries can help other countries develop. They might start new companies in developing countries or loan money to them. This type of *foreign investment* can bring jobs and new capital resources to a developing country. For example, many U.S. manufacturers have moved their factories to Mexico. This helps provide jobs for many Mexican workers. U.S. producers also benefit because labor and other production costs are lower in Mexico. But this situation can cause resentment among American workers who feel their jobs have been taken away.

NAFTA will make it easier for people in the U.S. to invest in Mexico.

Developing nations may also receive **foreign aid**. This help may be in the form of money, food, capital resources, or even military assistance. Recently, a group of developing countries asked that developed countries give at least 1 percent of their GDP to developing countries. Currently, many developed countries donate only about .15 percent.

Foreign aid is usually supplied by the governments of developed nations or the United Nations. During the 1960s, for example, a popular foreign-aid program called the Peace Corps was started in the United States. Scientists, teachers, health-care professionals, and others were sent by the U.S. government to foreign countries, usually developing nations. Sometimes they brought new types of farming or medical equipment with them. The Peace Corps volunteers then helped teach the people new skills to improve their standard of living.

In 1992, the United States contributed about $8.5 billion in non–military foreign aid to other countries. It provided about $6 billion in military aid.

An American Peace Corps volunteer teaches English to these children on the island of Luzon in the Philippines.

Economics Practice

Write answers to the following questions on a separate sheet of paper.

1. What is meant by foreign aid?

2. Give one reason why developed countries want to help developing countries.

3. How might banks aid developing countries?

Growing Pains of Developing Countries

Many developing countries use foreign investment and aid to develop industry. They hope that by becoming industrialized, they will produce more goods and services and improve their standard of living. Unfortunately, this is not always the case. For example, India has developed a steel industry. But India's production costs are several times higher than those in most other steel-producing countries. In other words, India does not have the comparative advantage in steel production. So Indians have to pay higher prices for steel.

The problems of overcrowding and extreme poverty are widespread in cities throughout the developing world. Millions of people who had been struggling to survive on subsistence farming have moved to the cities. There they hoped to find a new and better way of life. But in most cases, they weren't prepared for city jobs and city living. They found themselves caught between the old and new ways of life.

What are the solutions for developing countries? Some economists and government leaders say that developing countries should not change too rapidly. People need time to adjust to new technology and new ways of life. A developing nation should start by improving methods of small farming throughout the country. Along with this, the country should concentrate on improving human resources. This means better education and health care for the population. As people get used to new technology and improve their skills, the change to industry will come more naturally. A country will improve, change, and grow as its people do. And more people will benefit.

Some people also suggest that these countries develop a number of industries, not just one. This way a country will not be dependent on one product and the demand for it. This is especially true when that product is one in which the country does not have the comparative advantage. For example, Mexico put a great amount of money into its oil industry. But Mexico had trouble competing with Middle Eastern oil prices. This hurt its economy greatly. Now, Mexico is also developing a number of other industries to strengthen its economy. Vast sections of the country have been newly opened to tourism. And Mexico is rapidly expanding many areas of manufacturing.

Finally, developing countries should learn to use their resources in an environmentally sound way. Developed countries such as the United States have learned hard lessons about pollution and waste. Now they are having to spend valuable dollars to clean up the environment. By avoiding these mistakes, developing countries can use their existing resources in a healthier, more efficient way.

Economics Practice

Write answers to the following questions on a separate sheet of paper.

1. What is one problem experienced by developing countries?

2. What is one way that a developing country might help solve that problem?

Learn More About It:
The United Nations' Role in Developing Nations

The United Nations (U.N.) was founded in 1945. World War II had just ended. Government leaders believed that an international organization such as the U.N. would help avoid another bloody, destructive war.

Today, 159 nations belong to the U.N. Its main purposes are to:

- maintain international peace and security,
- develop friendly relations among nations, and
- help countries cooperate in solving economic, social, and human-rights problems.

The U.N. plays an active role in aiding developing countries. It provides foreign aid and sponsors conferences on problems in these countries. It promotes basic human rights, such as education and health, in all countries. U.N. members believe that by eliminating poverty and ignorance, they can bring about world peace.

Chapter Review

Chapter Summary

- Developed countries are usually highly industrialized. People in developed countries usually have a higher standard of living than those in other nations.

- Developing countries have less industry than developed countries. Their populations usually have a lower standard of living.

- In most developing countries, there is a low per capita GNP (under $2,000), a low literacy rate, poor health conditions, and a fast-growing population. More people in these countries make their living by farming than by working in industry.

- Developed countries often try to aid developing countries. Foreign banks might make loans to developing countries. And foreign businesses might start companies in those countries. This aids the growth of jobs and new capital resources.

- Foreign aid is often given to developing countries in the form of food, money, education, capital resources, or military help.

- As developing countries become more industrialized, they sometimes experience problems. Many families who live from subsistence farming head for the cities in search of a better life. They often have a hard time trying to make a living in the cities, which are already overcrowded.

- Some economists suggest that developing countries shouldn't change into industrial societies too rapidly. People need time to get used to new technology. Money should first be spent on improving small farming, education, and health care. Developing countries should also try to develop industries in which they have the comparative advantage. Finally, they should use their resources in an environmentally sound way.

Chapter Quiz

Write answers to the following questions on a separate sheet of paper.

A. Thinking About Economics

1. Which type of country has more industry, a developed or a developing country? Explain.

2. Which type of country has a higher standard of living, a developed or a developing country? Explain.

3. What is the difference in per capita GDP between a developing and a developed country?

4. How do most people in developing countries make a living?

5. Why are many people in developing countries unable to read and write?

6. What is health care like in many developing countries?

7. How might a rapidly growing population add to a developing country's problems?

8. How might banks or businesses in a developed country take part in developing a poorer country's resources?

9. What are three forms of foreign aid?

10. Explain what is meant by subsistence farming.

B. Personal Economics

Compare your life to that of a person in a developing country. In what ways might your life be different? You might think about education, health care, and job opportunities.

C. World Economics

The money that the United States spends in foreign aid to developing countries comes from U.S. taxpayers. This money could be spent in the United States instead. Do you think the United States should continue to give foreign aid? Why or why not?

Unit Eight Review

Write answers to the following questions on a separate sheet of paper.

1. What is the difference between imports and exports?

2. How does international trade benefit a country?

3. What is one problem that can occur in international trade?

4. What is a trade deficit?

5. What are two ways a government might restrict trade?

6. What are two main differences between developed and developing countries?

7. Describe health care and the literacy rate found in most developing countries.

8. How can a fast-growing population add to a developing country's problems?

9. Explain what is meant by per capita GDP.

10. What role does the Peace Corps play in developing countries?

Appendix

Glossary

Index

Glossary

agency shop a business in which employees are not required to join a union but must pay union dues

annually yearly

arbitration a process by which an outside party decides the terms of an agreement that must be accepted by both sides in a labor dispute

automation the use of machinery, often computerized, in place of human labor

bait and switch an illegal form of advertising

bank panic a situation in which many banks fail because they are not able to meet the demands of their depositors for cash

bankrupt unable to pay debts

bartering the direct exchange of one good or service for another without the use of money

Better Business Bureau a private organization that helps protect consumers from unfair business practices

board of directors a group of people elected by stockholders to make major decisions for a corporation

bond an IOU. The person who buys a *bond* is lending money to the government or corporation that sells the bond. The bondholder earns interest and is repaid at a specified date.

boycott a refusal to buy goods or services until an agreement is reached

budget a breakdown of how income is used; a personal plan for spending income

budget deficit a financial situation in which spending is greater than income or revenues

budget surplus a financial situation in which spending is less than income or revenues

business cycle alternating time periods of expanding and contracting economic activity

capital human-made things, such as machines and tools, that are used to produce goods and services

capital gain the money earned when you sell something for more than you paid for it

capital loss the money lost when you sell something for less than you paid for it

central bank a bank whose functions include controlling the nation's money supply

certificate of deposit (CD) a type of time-deposit savings account for a fixed amount of money with a higher fixed interest rate than most other savings accounts

chamber of commerce a group of representatives of local businesses who meet regularly to promote business in their town or city

charities non-profit organizations that accept donations such as money, goods, and volunteer time, and then provide aid to needy people

check clearing the process in which the Federal Reserve transfers checks and money between banks

circular flow of income the flow of payments for goods and services between households and businesses

closed shop a business that only hires workers who already belong to a union

collateral property or cash offered by a borrower as a guarantee that a loan will be repaid

collective bargaining a process by which management and labor reach agreements through negotiation and compromise

command system an economic system in which the government controls the production and distribution of goods and services

commercial banks banks that provide checking accounts and savings accounts, and make loans for a variety of purposes

common stock stock that gives the stockholder voting rights but may or may not offer dividends

comparative advantage a country's ability to produce a product at a lower opportunity cost than other countries

comparison shopping looking at similarities and differences in features, prices, and quality of competing goods or services

competition a situation in which producers or sellers of similar goods or services each try to get consumers to buy their products

complementary goods goods that are used with each other, such as cars and tires

compound interest interest earned on the deposit and on all previously earned interest

consumer a person who buys goods and services

Consumer Price Index (CPI) a statistic used to measure inflation

contraction a time period when GDP is decreasing

corporation a business that is owned by stockholders

cost-of-living raise a raise in income to keep wages even with inflation

cost of production costs of things such as natural resources, capital, and labor, which must be paid by producers

cost-push inflation the kind of inflation caused by the rising cost of resources such as labor or oil

counterfeit illegally reproduced; fake; for example, a *counterfeit* ten-dollar bill

credit the promise to pay later for the purchase of goods or services without the actual transfer of money

creditor a person or business who is owed money

credit union a kind of bank that is owned by members who belong to a certain company or group

currency coins and paper money

cyclical unemployment a situation that occurs when people are out of work because of a downturn in the business cycle

deflation a decrease in the average price of all goods and services

demand the amount of a good or service that consumers are willing and able to buy at different prices

demand curve the line on a graph that represents the amount of a good or service that consumers will buy at different prices

demand deposit account a checking account. Funds are payable on *demand* to the holder of the check.

demand-pull inflation the kind of inflation caused when consumer spending is greater than the amount of goods and services available

denominations units of value

depression a long-lasting and severe recession

developed countries countries that are highly industrialized and have a higher standard of living than developing countries

developing countries countries that depend mainly on agriculture instead of industry and have a lower standard of living than developed countries

discount rate the rate of interest charged by the Federal Reserve Bank to borrowing banks

dividend a share in a corporation's profit that is paid to a stockholder

durable lasting a long time without wearing out

economics the study of how people, businesses, and governments choose to use their limited resources

economic system the way that a country or culture produces and distributes goods and services

embargo a government policy that cuts off trade with certain countries

entrepreneurs people who come up with the ideas for producing goods and services. They are willing to take the risks of going into business.

equilibrium price the price at which the amount demanded equals the amount supplied

estate tax a tax on the property of a person who has died

excise tax a tax on certain items such as alcohol, tobacco, and gasoline

executives people responsible for directing and managing a business

expansion a time period when GDP is increasing

expenditures expenses

exports goods sold to other countries

factors of production the four things needed to produce goods and services: natural resources, labor, capital, and entrepreneurs

Federal Deposit Insurance Corporation (FDIC) a corporation that insures bank deposits up to $100,000

Federal Reserve System the name of the central bank of the United States

financial institutions banks, credit unions, savings and loans, and other organizations that offer services related to saving and borrowing money

fiscal policy the government program of increasing or decreasing taxes and government spending to control inflation and unemployment

fixed incomes incomes that do not change

foreign aid aid that one country gives to another in the form of money, capital resources, and food

franchise a business arrangement in which a large business chain, such as a fast food company, allows another person or group to operate an outlet using its name to sell goods or services

fraud deceit, trickery

free trade unrestricted trade between countries

frictional unemployment a situation that occurs when people are between jobs or are looking for their first jobs

fringe benefits any benefits given to workers other than wages, such as vacation pay, sick leave, pensions, and so forth

full warranty a warranty that promises to replace or repair all parts at no cost for a certain period of time

generic without a brand name

goods things that can be seen, touched, and bought or sold

government revenue tax dollars received by government

graph a diagram that shows the relationship between two or more sets of things

Gross Domestic Product (GDP) the total dollar value of the final goods and services produced in a country each year

import quota a law that sets a fixed amount of imports

imports goods bought from other countries

incentives things that encourage people to work harder or to produce more

income the amount of money that a person makes in a certain period of time

income tax a tax individuals pay on income above a certain amount and corporations pay on profits

infant mortality rate the percentage of infants who die during their first year

inflation an increase in the average price of all goods and services

inheritance tax a tax on inherited property or money

interchangeable capable of being put in place of one another

interest a specified amount of money a borrower must pay a lender for the use of borrowed funds

international trade trade between nations

intersect to cross at a point. The point on a graph where a supply curve and a demand curve *intersect* marks the equilibrium price.

inventory products that a business has in stock and ready to be sold

invest to use money to earn interest or income, or in the hopes of making a profit; for example, to buy stocks or bonds

investment the use of money to earn interest or income, or to make a profit. In economics, *investment* often means spending by a business on capital goods.

labor workers

labor force those 16 years old or older who are either employed or looking for work

labor union an organization that fights for workers' rights, wages, and benefits in a particular industry

laissez faire a basic policy that calls for non-interference by the government in business matters

law of demand the economic law which states that consumers will buy more of a good or service as the price goes down

law of supply the economic law which states that producers are willing to supply more of a good or service as the price becomes higher

life expectancy the number of years that an average person can expect to live

limited warranty a warranty that promises to pay all or partial replacement costs on certain parts for a specified period of time

literacy rate the percentage of people in a population who can read and write

lockout the closing of a business by management to force workers to accept terms of an agreement

losses what happens when a producer's total costs are greater than total revenues; the opposite of profits

market system an economic system in which individuals, not the government, control production and distribution of goods and services; also called *capitalism*

minimum wage the lowest hourly amount of money that a business can legally pay its workers

mixed system an economic system that includes both private ownership of property and government control of some services and industries

monetary policy the Federal Reserve Bank program of increasing or decreasing the money supply to control inflation and unemployment

money-market account a savings account that requires a large minimum deposit

money supply the value of all currency and checking account balances in a country

monopoly a business that has no competition; it produces a unique product or service

national debt the total amount of money owed by the federal government

natural resources things provided by nature, such as wood, oil, and coal, that can be used to produce goods and services

opportunity cost whatever is given up when a choice must be made; a trade-off

partnership a business that is owned by two or more people

peak the highest point in the business cycle

pension a regular payment to a retired person by his or her former employer

per capita GDP GDP of a country divided by the number of people in the population; a measure of a country's wealth compared to other countries

perfect competition a situation in which there are a large number of buyers and sellers for the same product; supply and demand determine price

portable easily carried or moved

poverty line the minimum yearly income that a family must have in order to meet its basic needs

preferred stock stock that offers the stockholder stated dividends but does not give the stockholder voting rights

prime rate the lowest rate of interest that banks offer their best business customers

principal in a loan, the original amount of money borrowed

priorities things that come first in order of importance

productivity the amount of goods and services produced by a worker or business in a given time period

profit the money made by a business after all costs have been paid

protectionism the policy of limiting trade with other countries to protect domestic industries

protective tariff a tax meant to raise the price of an imported good in order to protect a certain industry from foreign competition

real GDP GDP adjusted up or down to account for inflation

recession a time period when GDP decreases for two quarters (six months) in a row

reserve requirement the amount of money a bank must keep in its vault or on deposit at the Fed to back up its customer's deposits.

revenue money brought in by a business

revenue tariff an import tax used to provide government revenue

right-to-work laws state laws which give people the right to work without belonging to a union

robots electronic machines that are programmed to do tasks on an assembly line

sales tax a tax on purchases

scab laborers workers who cross a picket line to do the jobs of striking workers

scarcity not enough of a certain resource to satisfy people's needs and wants

seasonal unemployment   a situation that occurs when people are out of work for a part of the year because of the seasonal nature of their jobs

securities   stocks or bonds

service   an activity performed for others for money, such as teaching or selling

shortage   what happens when, at a given price, people want to buy more of a good or service than is available

social insurance programs   a variety of programs meant to prevent poverty. Social Security, worker's compensation, unemployment insurance, and Medicare are well-known examples. Workers pay into these programs while they are employed.

social welfare programs programs that provide income, housing, and health insurance to the individuals and families who cannot work

sole proprietorship   a business owned by one person

specialization   the use of resources to produce only a single or a few kinds of goods or services

standard of living   a way to measure how well the needs and wants of citizens are being met by a country's economic system

statistics   figures that are collected to get information about a particular subject; numerical data

stock   a share of ownership in a corporation

stockbroker   a person who is licensed to buy and sell stocks and bonds for other people

stockholder   a person who buys stock in a corporation; shareholder

stock market   a place where stocks and bonds are traded (bought and sold)

strike   a work stoppage by labor to win terms of an agreement

structural unemployment   a situation that occurs when people are out of work because they lack the skills or education necessary for available jobs

subsistence farming   farming that produces enough food for the farming family to live on, but nothing more

substitute goods   goods that can take the place of one another

supply   the amount of a good or service that producers are willing and able to produce at different prices

supply curve   the line on a graph that represents the amount of a good or service that producers are willing to supply at different prices

supply-side economics the belief that high unemployment and inflation can be solved by encouraging people and businesses to produce more

surplus what happens when, at a given price, more of a good or service is available than people want to buy

tariff a tax on imports

technology the use of science to create new or better goods and services or more efficient methods of production

time-deposit account a savings account that requires money to be left in the account for a certain period of time

trade deficit a condition in which the value of a nation's imports is greater than the value of its exports

trade surplus a condition in which the value of a nation's exports is greater than the value of its imports

traditional system an economic system based on past ways of life and culture

trough the lowest point in the business cycle

unemployment rate the percentage of people in the labor force who are looking for work but have not found jobs

union dues dues paid by workers to support the union

union shop a business at which employees must join the union after a certain period of time, usually 60 or 90 days

utility companies businesses that provide vital services such as electricity, natural gas, and water; they are often government-regulated monopolies

wages the price that businesses pay workers in exchange for labor

warranty a written guarantee that products or services do what they are supposed to do

withdraw to take out

Index